P9-DDS-955
NED!
at
Ned's
Bar
Mitzvah
April 13
1986
KENNY
Michael
Mr. Kenneth Stolman
Table 15
JEWISH
BAR MITZVAH FAVORITES
BENJAMIN
Ryan Leib
A
Bar Mitzvah
Journal
LAUREN'S
13th
RECORD
HOP
ROCK YOUR FEET
TO
LEIGH'S DISCO BEAT
MAY 4, 1986
BAR-MITZVAH
Congratulations
BRETT'S BAR MITZVAH
DECEMBER 7, 1991
For Your
BAR MITZVAH
CHOCOLATE GOURMETS OF AMERICA
LONDONS ONE HUNDRED
KEN
Sandy

BAR MITZVAH DISCO

BAR MITZVAH DISCO

The Music May Have Stopped, but the Party's Never Over

Roger Bennett
Jules Shell
Nick Kroll

Crown Publishers/New York

Julie Hermelin
9.5.80
Southfield, Michigan

Published in the United States by Crown Publishers, an imprint of the Crown Publishing Group, a division of Random House, Inc., New York.
www.crownpublishing.com

Crown is a trademark and the Crown colophon is a registered trademark of Random House, Inc.

Library of Congress Cataloging-in-Publication Data is available upon request

ISBN 1-4000-8044-4

Printed in China

Design by Kay Schuckhart/Blond on Pond
Photograph on page 6 by Aaron Cobbett

10 9 8 7 6 5 4 3 2 1

First Edition

To all the mothers across the globe who entrusted us with their precious family albums, especially ours, Val, Lynn, and Joan.

FOREWORD

BY THE VILLAGE PEOPLE

When we were asked to write the foreword to this book, we were both honored and a little confused. First of all, while we are all artists with a wide array of creative talents, none of us is an author. Second, none us had had a Bar Mitzvah. Third, not one of us is even Jewish. But then it all began to make sense. Music can make you laugh, and it can make you cry, but our music—as much as anyone else's—has become synonymous with the word P-A-R-T-Y. "Y.M.C.A." makes you want to burn up the dance floor; indeed, the writers of this book claim that it is the most important song to hit the Jewish religion since "Hava Nagilah." Now, we don't want to go that far, but we will say that we are so glad to have contributed something that people can always enjoy—that summons up family and friends and the celebration of life.

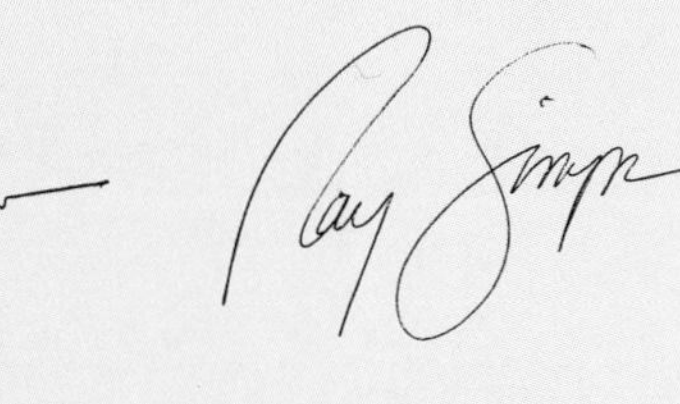

JEWISH TELEGRAPH

Their big day

● BARMITZVAH at Childwall Synagogue on Shabbat was Roger Bennett, younger son of Valerie and Ivor Bennett, of Calderstones. Roger is the grandchild of Flora Bennett of Liverpool and the late Abe Bennett and Rita and Sam Polak of Liverpool. He has an elder brother, Nigel, 15 and a younger sister Amy, 10 months.

A pupil at Liverpool College where he is chairman of the Debating Society Junior Section, Roger has represented Liverpool at chess and his other interests include reading, tennis, golf, cricket and collecting records.

His father, Mr Ivor Bennett is chairman of the Merseyside Amalgamated Talmud Torah.

Joan and Stephen Shell announce the Bat Mitzvah of their daughter, **Julie Dianna,** on Saturday, April 21 at 9:00 a.m.

Julie is a seventh grade student at the Bexley Junior High and Tifereth Israel Religious Schools. She received her Bat Mitzvah training from Cantor Jack Chomsky and Dotan Herszage.

Julie will be participating in a proxy Bat Mitzvah for Irina Kiseleva of the U.S.S.R. Because Irina's family has been denied exit visas, Julie will dedicate a portion of her Torah reading to her Soviet Twin. It is Julie's hope that Irina may obtain freedom so that she may come to understand and appreciate her Jewish heritage. The Twinning Ceremony is sponsored by Women's American ORT.

Julie is the granddaughter of Mr. and Milton Adler, Great Neck, N.Y.; Ruth Shell and the late Max Shell of Columbus; and the great granddaughter of Esther Adler of Tamarac, Florida.

Joan, Steve, Julie, Eileen, and Debbie invite their friends, relatives and members of the Congregation to worship with them on this happy occasion and join them for kiddush immediately following services.

INTRODUCTION

This book has everything and nothing to do with Bar and Bat Mitzvahs at the same time. It is as much about the particular experiences of our generation that we have previously left to languish in suburban rec rooms and the darker recesses of our memories—the unmistakable smell of the smoke machine, the cotton-poly feel of a Benetton rugby shirt, and the sound of a Lionel Richie—as it is about ritual, candle lighting, or memory glasses. This is a generational telling in the words and pictures of those that lived it large, a coming-of-age story, a cultural history, and an unabashed celebration of style, or to be honest, the lack thereof.

The Bar Mitzvah is an age-old rite of passage. It is also a crafty sleight of hand—a brilliant attempt to persuade thirteen-year-olds to ignore the trauma of their early teens by unilaterally proclaiming them to be fully-fledged men and women overnight. This, despite all credible evidence suggesting otherwise: mouths full of braces, faces ripe with acne, and the fact that puberty may still be light-years away.

In modern times, this ritualized act of self-deception has become a parallel universe, two parts Fantasy Island to one part Vegas, rife with its gorgeous girls, piles of cash, and hastily scribbled thank-you notes. An examination of this evolution is an examination of who we are and how we got to be this way. With a future so uncertain, it has become more critical than ever that we retrace our steps and understand the forces that have shaped our identities, families, communities, and culture. The people represented in the pages of this book came of age in contradictory times mostly during the late seventies, eighties, and early nineties. We believed the labels we wore said as much about us as the words that came out of our mouths. We did our damnedest to get to third base despite the backdrop of the deadly scourge of AIDS. Greed was good yet we still learned all the words to "We Are the World." And, our propensity to steal Screwdrivers and Marlboro Reds from the bar was primarily motivated by the First Lady's desperate demand that we "Just Say No."

Now that the memories of our formative years have marinated, there is no better place to look than the Bar Mitzvah circuit for a glimpse of self-understanding. If you are Jewish—or if you had a Jew or two in your class—there would have been a golden year in this time span when it seemed like you attended a Bar Mitzvah party almost weekly. Each one was like a peewee Studio 54, filled with style, music, lust, and excess. History will mark as one of our generation's great achievements the ascension of the Bar Mitzvah to its rightful place among the pantheon of other such universally beloved rituals as St. Patrick's Day and Cinco de Mayo. As we write this book, two of the country's most reliable news sources, *The Wall Street Journal* and *People* magazine, have dedicated stories to the growing phenomenon of non-Jews who enjoyed their Bar and Bat Mitzvah experiences to such an extent that they threw them for their own kids in places such as New Jersey (understandable, perhaps) and Texas (logic defying).

When we originally contemplated this phenomenon, we put it to the test by bringing it up in conversations among our friends, Jewish or not. We watched as their normally languid faces lit up while remembering their own Bar and Bat Mitzvah experiences. It quickly became clear: We had to expand our reach. We set up a website in the fall of 2003 to cajole first our families, then our friends, and before long, complete and utter strangers, to tell their stories and share their memories. Photographs and stories flowed in by the thousands. These memories were once an individual source of shame, but thanks to the healing powers of time and a growing appreciation of nostalgia, it appears that these golden nuggets of memory can now be appreciated for what they truly are.

Welcome to *Bar Mitzvah Disco.* A journey from a more innocent age to a time of unabashed materialism, all lived with an insufficient dose of irony. This journey consists of a coming-of-age story mired in one of the most awkward periods of life, a story of style that makes it seem like the full-length mirror was only invented in 1992, and a cultural history based on the fact that Bar Mitzvahs have saved more entertainment careers than the cabaret circuit in Branson, Missouri. These themes are composed of a series of interconnected and complicated stories represented within the move from the city to the suburb; the evolution of class and race; the hunger for idealized community in the sixties shifting to a celebration of the individual in the seventies and eighties; the evolving role and relevance of ritual and religion in our everyday lives; the rise and rise of popular and consumer culture; and the changing structure of the modern American family.

We would be remiss if we failed to pay appropriate respect to two sets of people without whom this book would not have been possible. First of all, we tip our hats to the beautiful mothers of North America, the keepers of family stories and the guardians of 97 percent of Bar Mitzvah photograph albums still in circulation. You believed us when we promised that we would treat your pleather and Lucite treasures as if they were our own. And because of your trust, this collection was able to see the light of day.

Second, we stand in awe of all the Bar Mitzvah photographers who have dedicated their creative lives to perfecting the art form we have fallen so hopelessly in love with. Art history has not recorded the name of the underappreciated genius who first gave us the "holy scholar shot" and the classic "gentle wave goodbye." This book is a collection of your work—both the formal shots of family and friends, and the candids that say so much. Indeed, the format of our book faithfully follows the running order of the traditional Bar Mitzvah album you have defined over the decades, which so artfully follows the flow and climax of the ritual and celebration.

Almost all of the albums that flooded in from all points were accompanied by handwritten disclaimers along the lines of "Here are my photographs. Nothing special here. Use as much as you want. We love the project." More often than not, the albums contained images of small girls riding into their Bat Mitzvahs on elephants, or awkward teens forced to pose in trees, in the back of Corvettes, or with hackneyed celebrity impersonators. Well, we have made a book out of it, and we invite you to revisit your favorite public rite of passage—however excruciating it may have been at the time—knowing you have made it through, hopefully unscathed. It is our hope that as we present the lives we have lived thus far, via your photos and your words, unvarnished, unfiltered, and straight from the source, they will act as an opportunity for all of us to ask ourselves: who are we, what are we inheriting, and what does it mean to us?

Roger Bennett, Jules Shell, Nick Kroll
New York City
www.barmitzvahdisco.com

Sara Solfanelli
3.31.90
Scranton, Pennsylvania

WISHING (IF I HAD A PHOTOGRAPH OF YOU)

It's not the way you look,
It's not the way that you smile.
—A Flock of Seagulls

The Bar and Bat Mitzvah experience thrust the individual young man or woman into the spotlight whether they were ready for the attention or not. So, it is no surprise that almost every album starts off with a formal portrait, capturing the youth in that au naturel, candid moment—taking a break from a hectic schedule to pose in a tree, sniff a flower, gaze at naval maneuvers, or pull off that difficult-to-wear fedora.

This is the moment where the photographer begins to develop his relationship with his model, so the shots are often tentative, and the subjects are at their most vulnerable and pliable. Though not as naked as the day they were born, some of the individuals look as comfortable as if that were the case. Like lab rats at the outset of an experiment, they are aware of their imminent induction into adulthood, though not entirely sure what is about to hit them. Others appear more ready to assume the burden of middle age; dressed like mini-corporate raiders or one of Charlie's Angels, they have waited a whole thirteen years of their lives for this moment.

"On the day of my Bar Mitzvah I suited up in my three-piece pinstriped and blew my hair out to the side and I felt like I was gonna be sick."

Todd Rosenberg
9.11.82
New Rochelle, New York

Michelle Shapiro
11.2.86
Battleground Country Club
Freehold, New Jersey

Lacey Schwartz
8.23.90
Seasons Restaurant
Woodstock, New York

Alicia Post
5.11.91
West Hemstead, New York

Stacy Marcus
5.26.90
Wayne, New Jersey

Jeremy Kroll
4.28.84
Rye, New York

"Bar Mitzvahs rock conceptually. A kid is about to go through puberty and get completely whacked out of synch, having urges they don't understand, desires and new ideas about the world. So what do we do? The whole community comes together and says . . . you're cool, go for it."

David Measer
5.5.84
Chasen's Restaurant
Hollywood, California

"The suit I was wearing was made for me by my uncle Arnold. I chose a suit cut like one of the ex-presidents of my synagogue. These were really distinguished men with gray hair, top hats, and navy blue three-piece pinstripe suits. My dad gave me his late mother's watch for the day. She wore it around her neck but I wore it across the belly. I was 13 going on 75."

Jamie Glassman
1.28.84
Hale Village
Cheshire, England

THE JEWISH BEE GEES

When you cross the city limits into Long Island, there should be a sign that says, "Welcome to Long Island, Bar Mitzvah Capital, USA." Writing a book on the subject of Bar Mitzvahs without citing Long Island is akin to writing about country music and neglecting to mention Nashville. And so, we pay homage to the area through the medium of one of our favorite families, the Weinbergs. Their photographs on this and the following four pages tell stories of brotherhood, of the evolution from boys to young men, and most importantly, of the modern history of the three-piece suit. It is for these reasons that we celebrate them, as well as because they obeyed the photographer's commands to a tee—whether it was to gently caress a birch tree or meditate studiously upon the holy scrolls. The Bar Mitzvah is all about manhood. And the Weinberg boys have more than their fair share of that attribute.

Josh Weinberg
9.29.79
Long Island, New York

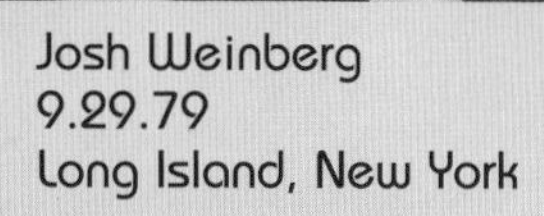

Josh Weinberg
9.29.79
Long Island, New York

Matt Weinberg
6.14.77
Long Island, New York

Matt Weinberg
6.14.77
Long Island, New York

"This was the last stand for my family as we knew it, as Mom and Dad separated a year later on their way to a divorce."

Doug Herzog
6.3.72
Paterson, New Jersey

IT'S A FAMILY AFFAIR

Both kids are good to Mom,
blood's thicker than mud.
—Sly & the Family Stone

The Bar Mitzvah experience is so much more than a celebration of one young person's passage into adulthood. It is also about the family they were embarrassed to be a part of. The portrait of the family was as compulsory an element of the Bar Mitzvah album as the starched smiles in unison they depicted.

But these shots are more than just the dominant reason architects were compelled to design a large space above the electric fireplace in the modern American home. They are a prism through which we can examine the changing face of the normative family structure. Thinly veiled beneath the desperate efforts to pull off vaguely Semitic Rockwellian poses, a revolution was occurring. This was the era in which marriages began to become disposable and our role models were less the idealized relationships of the Keatons and the Cosbys and more like Ike and Tina's, Sonny and Cher's, or Roseanne and Dan's. On the odd occasion they could even end up living the life depicted in *My Two Dads.*

So the Bar/Bat Mitzvah was the time when the child would not just be forced to navigate the family dysfunction, but could actually call the shots and decide which part of the event they would spend with Dad's side of the party, and which side with Mom's. Decode the dynamics at play in each shot for yourself, and appreciate the representations of machismo with Dad, blind adoration with Mom, and the times when the pretense was dropped altogether and the pets were wheeled in to replace the humans.

Mark Melnick
6.5.71
Aperion Manor, Kings Highway
Brooklyn, New York

Michael Larsen
5.27.73
Regency House
Queens, New York

Matt Weinberg
6.14.77
Long Island, New York

Jordana Winton
8.73
Huntington Towne House
Huntington, New York

THE SCARLET HEBREW LETTER

By AJ JACOBS

I never had a Bar Mitzvah. Well, not a real one. In college, my Jewish friends took pity on my Bar Mitzvah-less soul and threw me a surprise Bar Mitzvah party, complete with the ancient Semitic ritual of dancing to Kool and the Gang's "Celebration." But as for the bonafide Bar Mitzvah, nothing. Bubkes. The problem was, my family had assimilated with a vengeance. No seders, no dreidels, no hamantaschen. The closest we came to Jewish culture was the occasional poppy seed bagel, though even then we referred to the pink stuff on top by its New Testament name of "smoked salmon."

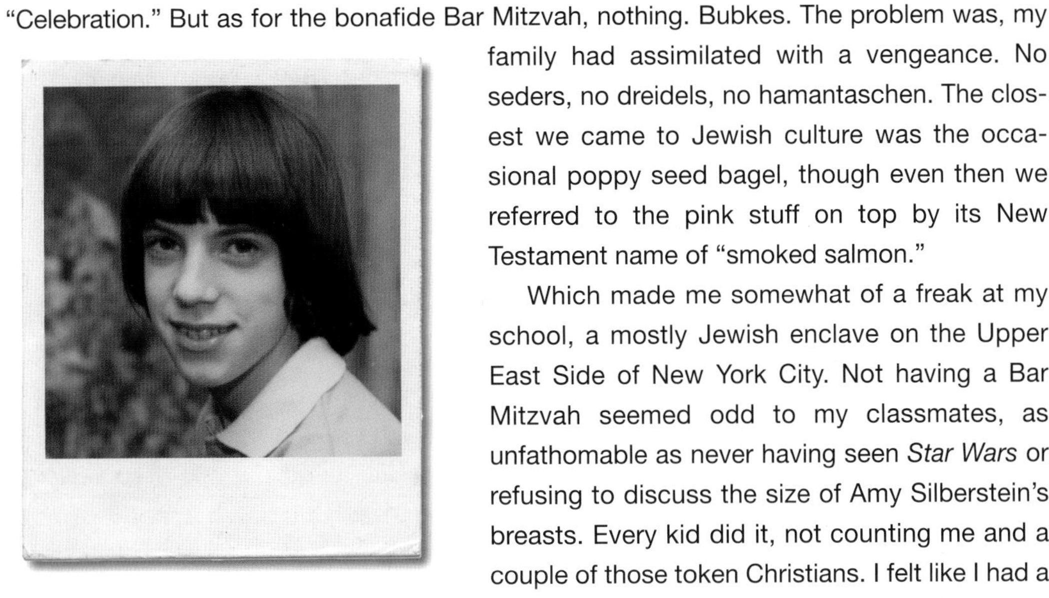

Which made me somewhat of a freak at my school, a mostly Jewish enclave on the Upper East Side of New York City. Not having a Bar Mitzvah seemed odd to my classmates, as unfathomable as never having seen *Star Wars* or refusing to discuss the size of Amy Silberstein's breasts. Every kid did it, not counting me and a couple of those token Christians. I felt like I had a scarlet aleph on my forehead. Not only would I never become a man, but I missed out on a couple thousand dollars of checks and several attractive fountain pens.

Even worse, every other weekend, I had to put on my ill-fitting blue blazer and khakis and go watch other thirteen-year-old boys get their moment in the spotlight with the challah and the kiddush cup. The parties were tolerable. I could do a respectable limbo. I had the requisite eye of the tiger on the dance floor. But the ceremonies? Those were as dull and meaningless as a foreign movie without subtitles.

Which is why I finally took emergency measures at Steve Levine's bar mitzvah. I arrived late to the temple and sat in the back. In my blazer pocket I had stashed Steve's gift, a handheld computer game, sort of a Paleolithic Gameboy with only one game: a little man who juggled several fast-moving balls. Smartly, I had forgotten to wrap the present. As the rabbi droned on about Steve's Torah portion, I thought maybe I should just make sure the batteries work. I wouldn't want to give Steve a battery-less game, right?

I slipped the video game into my Deuteronomy to hide it. I flipped the switch. Yep, the power works. Good.

"Misheberach avotenu," the rabbi said.

Maybe I should just see if the game isn't malfunctioning. Wouldn't want to give a broken game to Steve, right? I press Go. The balls start juggling.

Bleep, bleep, *Vchol tamid oo vchol shaa,* bleep, bleep. I dropped the ball. Dammit!

A woman turned around. She seemed confused. She thought she heard something bleep. I gave her a solemn head nod, trying to indicate how impressed I was with Steve's recitation of the haftarah. She turned back and I pressed Go again.

Bleep, bleep, bleep. A whole rash of balls. I was cooking. Bleep, bleep, bleep! *Splat.* I looked up. Several rows of Steve's relatives were staring at me. They were not pleased. They looked like they wanted to sacrifice me on a mountaintop. I shrugged my shoulders innocently and held up the cover of the Old Testament, which shielded my video game. They weren't fooled.

"Shhhhhh!!!!"

"That is not appropriate young man!"

"A shonda!"

After that, I learned my lesson. I only played my juggling game during the loud singing portions.

Those were not my best moments as a Jew. And come to think of it, I probably should have been sacrificed on the mountaintop. But I will say this. Bar Mitzvahs were my first real taste of being a minority. I was the alien, the other. And even I, the boy who never saw the inside of a Hebrew school, knew that being the outsider is a key part of the Jewish experience. So I got that going for me.

Adam Smith
11.5.83
Ridgeway Country Club
White Plains, New York

"These are my two shitzus, Mopsy and Flopsy. Better known as Shitty and Pissy."

Doug Herzog
6.3.72
Paterson, New Jersey

"My mom loved the dog so much, it had to be in the photo. She was a Maltese named Lambchop after Shari Lewis's sock puppet from the sixties television show that our parents used to watch."

Samantha and Jennifer Corwin
3.2.90
Rye Brook, New York

Ari Osur
6.13.87
Fairfield Sheraton
Fairfield, New Jersey

"The hotel where my reception was to be held had recently renovated its catering hall with brown wallpaper and drapes. My mother thought we should match our tuxedos to that color. She called it an 'earth-tone dress theme.'"

Ben Mittman
12.5.81
Washington Hotel and Beach
Belle Harbor, New York

Michael Larsen
5.27.73
Regency House
Jamaica, Queens, New York

LOSING MY RELIGION

That's me in the corner
That's me in the spotlight
—R.E.M.

A little known fact about Bar and Bat Mitzvahs is that in addition to the party, there is also a religious element to the event. The iconic image of the youth as a holy scholar is to Bar and Bat Mitzvahs what the multiple exposure shot is to the photographer's repertoire—misunderstood and underappreciated.

Assimilated? I don't think so. Almost every individual was able to temporarily overcome the fact that they could only read Hebrew phonetically, and pull off a mildy convincing impression of a learned sage of yore. Or at the very least, to look like they had just spent a taxing day as an extra on the set of *Yentl.* Indeed, some families were so overcome by the Holy Spirit they felt compelled to demonstrate some big air in front of the Holy Scriptures. We leave plenty of room for this section, partly because the images are quite remarkable, and partly to serve as a reminder of why we were supposedly meant to be there in the first place. Note the photo where the pretense of holding onto a sacred text has been dropped altogether and the Bar Mitzvah is left to piously cling onto an empty VHS video box.

"A lot of Catholic kids were having confirmation and were making no dough. I had a lot of Jewish friends who were getting paid from these parties and I was like damn, let's make some dough. Let's throw a Bar Mitzvah. I'd never been to synagogue. I did not know what the format was. Man, I just was out there with the outfit playing the role."

Aaron Judah Bondaroff
3.17.90
New York, New York

"Basic hair etiquette demanded the higher the poof on the dress, the higher the hair. To be sure there was no cause for concern, we invited my hairdresser to the party. There is nothing in life that a big round brush, a can of Aqua Net, and Richie from Cityslickers can't handle."

Sarra Cooper
5.18.91
Middle Bay Country Club
Oceanside, New York

"I designed my dress myself after seeing the Huey Lewis 'Stuck With You' video (the one where he is stranded on a desert island with a beautiful woman). I fell in love with the gown she was wearing, particularly the tall, puffy sleeves."

Rebecca Rubenstein
10.11.86
The Shadow Brooke
Shrewsbury, New Jersey

GRANDMA'S DOWN

By WENDY SPERO

Sadly, my grandmother stole the spotlight at my Bat Mitzvah.

I "became a woman" at the most reform temple of all time. One winter I could have sworn there was a small Christmas tree in the lobby. My service was to be a mere thirty-five minutes. I didn't have to write a speech about why the day was so special, I didn't have to learn another alphabet, and I didn't even have to rehearse. I showed up ten minutes before the congregation and the cantor told me where I was going to sit and what I was going to read: a small paragraph written in English Hebrew: "Boruch Atah Adonoy." Sweet. I get to be the center of attention. I get to be praised. And all I gotta do is wear my cool jappy dress from Betsy Johnson, slip on my mom's 1950's white gloves, which (for some unknown reason) she thought would "make the outfit," and show up.

The ceremony begins and when the time is right I stand and read aloud the Hebrew words—struggling with some of them on purpose to pretend that I'm actually translating something. I finish, sit down, and the rabbi compliments me on my hard work. I seem learned as all hell. I am a Jewish, bilingual, stylish, eighties pixie wearing gloves from the fifties. A true rock star.

But then the rabbi announces, "Will everyone in mourning, please rise." And my grandparents decide to STAND UP. *Twelve years* after my father's unexpected death, they decide to rise and make a profound statement about their loss. This was not out of character for my grandparents. They were particularly obsessed with my father and his death and brought him up as often as possible. Growing up, they consistently called me by *his name,* "by mistake." My grandmother can't deal, so as she stands up, she *faints* and falls to the ground. I have this on tape. It's actually really funny. Because there is this boring Jewish ceremony and then . . . all of a sudden . . . Grandma's DOWN.

My mom and I are up on the stage in total shock. We are obviously concerned, but because she faints on a regular basis, we know she'll be fine (and she was—she was very upbeat at the after party. She just had an ice pack attached to her head.) We were more surprised that my grandparents had really gone as far as to make a spectacle of their mourning on this day. *My* day, goddammit. In front of a congregation who knew their son had died twelve years ago and who knew how devastating that was for them.

Anyway, there's nothing like an old person falling over to spice things up at a boring religious service. Havoc ensues. Yelling and running between the aisles. The rabbi is clearly caught off guard but pulls it together and yelps out an authoritative: "Everyone remain calm. We are getting help!" Within minutes paramedics arrive and carry Grandma out on a stretcher. People settle down. There is a slight murmur in the crowd but the service awkwardly resumes.

It's obviously *very* sad that my grandparents lost their son (and that I lost my father). It's sad that they felt a need to have that be an integral part of my Bat Mitzvah. It's sad that I was so mad at my grandparents for taking the attention off me and my perfectly executed fake Hebrew delivery. It's sad that I was forced to wear white gloves. But perhaps what's most sad is that the idiot videographer shut off the camera upon Grandma's impact to the ground. So the whole paramedic part was never captured on film.

"My father decided that a thirteen-year-old boy shouldn't have facial hair when he becomes a man. He made my mother wax my upper lip. Certain parts of the mustache never grew back. I know my father meant well, but waxing is not appropriate for young men, unless they live in certain parts of South Beach."

Andrew Goldberg
3.7.91
Mamaroneck Beach & Yacht Club
Mamaroneck, New York

David and Jono Kohan
4.16.77
Los Angeles, California

Ari Osur
6.13.87
Fairfield Sheraton
Fairfield, New Jersey

Eric Rubenstein
2.25.84
Tamarac, Florida

Jason C. Silverman
August 1984
Edmonton, Alberta, Canada

MEATBALLS 13

By ERIC DRYSDALE

I was Bar Mitzvahed on a steamy summer afternoon in an outdoor chapel of low wooden benches on the bank of a small New Hampshire lake. Nearby water-skiers threatened to drown out my haftarah, as mosquitoes nipped at friends and family under swaying eaves of oak.

This was the site of worship at the Jewish summer camp I attended for eight years of my childhood and early adolescence. The decision to be Bar Mitzvahed there was a simple one. It was at Camp Tel Hai where my parents had met fifteen years earlier. Dad was the head of the drama department, while Mom was a boating instructor, and his muse. I spent my first summer there as an infant in 1969.

By the time I was of Bar Mitzvah age, my father was fast climbing in a career in Jewish social service, and had already moved the family around the country several times, from New England to Tennessee and on to Ohio. My summer camp had become an important and rare constant in my life. Not surprisingly, I felt far more connected to my Jewish self there than at my newly adopted Reform congregation in Akron. Even at age thirteen, I suspected that a synagogue at which people were not permitted to wear a yarmulke was somewhat beyond Reform, and rather closer to Presbyterianism.

So, after studying at home in Ohio, and then working with the camp's resident Torah scholar, I was brought to lead the prayers as part of the regular outdoor Shabbat service. The only difference this Saturday was the row of folding chairs at the back of the clearing to accommodate visitors. A kid-sized Torah scroll was taken from a fancy plywood box—an "ark" most likely built and decorated by counselors from a previous summer's woodworking shop. I adjusted the gooseneck on the tiny portable PA system with a crackle, and tentatively sang my haftarah.

The cantor for the ceremony was an older camper I barely knew. He wore his superior ability to read Hebrew and lead a service with a snottiness more appropriate for an arrogant youth tennis champ—which he also happened to be. I distinctly remember my entry into manhood being greeted with condescending eye rolls from him each time I missed a note or even slightly mispronounced a word.

The reception that followed the service was roughly the same as any other Shabbat at the camp, except for the substitution of too-sweet wine for the usual too-sweet grape juice.

In addition to my Bar Mitzvah, I have fond memories of my summer alma mater. The camp did its best to situate its curriculum between American and Jewish culture, a strategy which came with an inevitable dose of cognitive dissonance. The powers that were saw no irony in programming a night of counselor Jell-O wrestling within a couple of days of a somber Holocaust memorial observance, complete with mandatory screenings of the Holocaust documentary *Night and Fog.*

Perhaps that's as it should be. As the grandson of survivors myself, I've always been taught that every person who can stand up and say, "I'm proud to be a Jew," is one the Nazis didn't get. I am definitely proud to be a Jew. If my fond memories of Miriam Zalinsky's boob slipping out during Jell-O wrestling had some subconscious influence on that, then the American Jewish experiment is working, though in weirder ways than anyone could have possibly expected.

Kate Lee
5.19.90
Warren, New Jersey

Rodger Kohn
9.8.78
Baton Rouge, Louisiana

Doug Herzog
6.3.72
Paterson, New Jersey

Jim Cone
10.13.79
Wayne, New Jersey

Mike Epstein
5.29.89
Columbus, Ohio

Jon Kesselman
1.16.88
North Hollywood, California

Julie Hermelin
9.5.80
Southfield, Michigan

Asher Weinberg
12.12.81
Woodbury Country Club
Long Island, New York

MAN IN THE MIRROR

Take a look at yourself
and then make that . . . change!
—Michael Jackson

Mirror, mirror on the wall, who is the most pubescent of them all? Although many of us now try and claim we had no idea what we were wearing, the classic mirror shot says otherwise. The mirror preening was often preceded by a few private minutes spent practicing the Running Man in socks and underpants. But then the photographer was let into the room, and these images are the result.

Today, as we look at these shots, we are struck with that same sense of awe that first charmed the likes of Narcissus, the self-admirer. Perhaps what tickles our fancy is seeing two images of the same person, one real and one reflected. Maybe it is that every mirror ever used in this photographic genre had a heavy golden frame that looked as if it had been pried directly from the walls of the Regal Beagle. The mirror shot allows our gaze to fall voyeuristically upon the subjects, who are like bullfighters about to enter the ring, forced to consider their own mortality.

Anonymous
circa 1968
Queens, New York

"I was a giant pair of lips attached to gangly legs, topped off by my huge, naturally curly hair, with an enormous bow. I looked like a Q-tip. As a public service, my parents should have kept me indoors."

Jill Barnett
5.2.87
Winding Hollow Country Club
Columbus, Ohio

"I thought if I wore white, in addition to becoming a man, I might just lose my virginity that day as well."

Matthew Issembert
6.6.92
Washington, D.C.

99 RED BALLOONS

99 red balloons
Floating in the summer sky
—Nena

For thousands of years, the ritual of youth being called to the Torah sufficed. But in the late sixties, all of that began to change. If the Bar or Bat Mitzvah was to be truly memorable, it had to have a theme. And we are not talking about the theme of happy family and loyal friends coming together to enjoy one special little (wo)man's entrance into adulthood. Themes had to be inspired by the thirteen-year-old's unique passions . . . from the Beatles, to Indiana Jones, Latinos, or Tweety Bird. On the odd occasion, the celebrant was cut out of the equation altogether, as Mom chose her dress first and then a theme with a color scheme to match it.

So, savor the empty room, or rather, the calm before the storm. Before the party began, before the guests shuffled in, before the band or DJ filled the room with song, the reception room lay empty. It waited anxiously, gussied up with complex lighting systems, hidden confetti cannons, and melting ice sculptures. An imaginary world prepared to transport the guests to their wildest fantasies for one night only, be that the chicest of nightclubs, the toniest of beach resorts, or a large synagogue catering hall decked out with a couple of sombreros and a multicolored balloon arch.

Joshua Speisman
11.25.89
Roslyn, New York

Stephanie Huttner
2.28.87
The Fairmont Hotel
Denver, Colorado

Anonymous
Circa 1967

Andrew Waranch
5.28.88
Woodholme Country Club
Baltimore, Maryland

Andrew Waranch
5.28.88
Woodholme Country Club
Baltimore, Maryland

Matt Wood
3.15.86
The Palladium
New York, New York

Sarra Cooper
5.18.91
Middle Bay Country Club
Oceanside, New York

DON'T YOU FORGET ABOUT ME

As you walk on by,
Will you call my name?
—Simple Minds

What parenting technique is guaranteed to repair your child's shattered self-confidence, clarify sexual confusion, and convey the sense of love you cannot quite bring yourself to communicate directly? That would be a forty-foot sign with your child's name on it proclaiming the supreme power of the word "Ned" or "Lauren" for all the world to see.

To be sure, these signs played an important functional as well as emotional role at each event. They were a constant reminder to guests, some of them as distant as third cousin twice removed, and all of whom had been to twelve similar events in the previous couple of weeks, exactly whose Bar or Bat Mitzvah they were actually attending. In a more Machiavellian way, they served as a subliminal reminder to all of whom the checks should be made payable to.

Elliott Goldkind
10.8.77
Queens, New York

"I didn't run into anyone from the Mark Rosenthal Bar Mitzvah luncheon that is listed on the board below my name, but I did get a kick out of the Christian event that was also listed. That is classic St. Louis, right there."

Amy Tobin
8.23.86
St. Louis, Missouri

"Reagan was in office. The real estate market hadn't crashed yet. I got a Discman, a VCR, and I didn't have to go to Hebrew school ever again. Things were good. I feel sorry for all those people who had theirs in '91 to '94: recession-era Bar Mitzvahs."

Andrew Waranch
5.28.88
Woodholme Country Club
Baltimore, Maryland

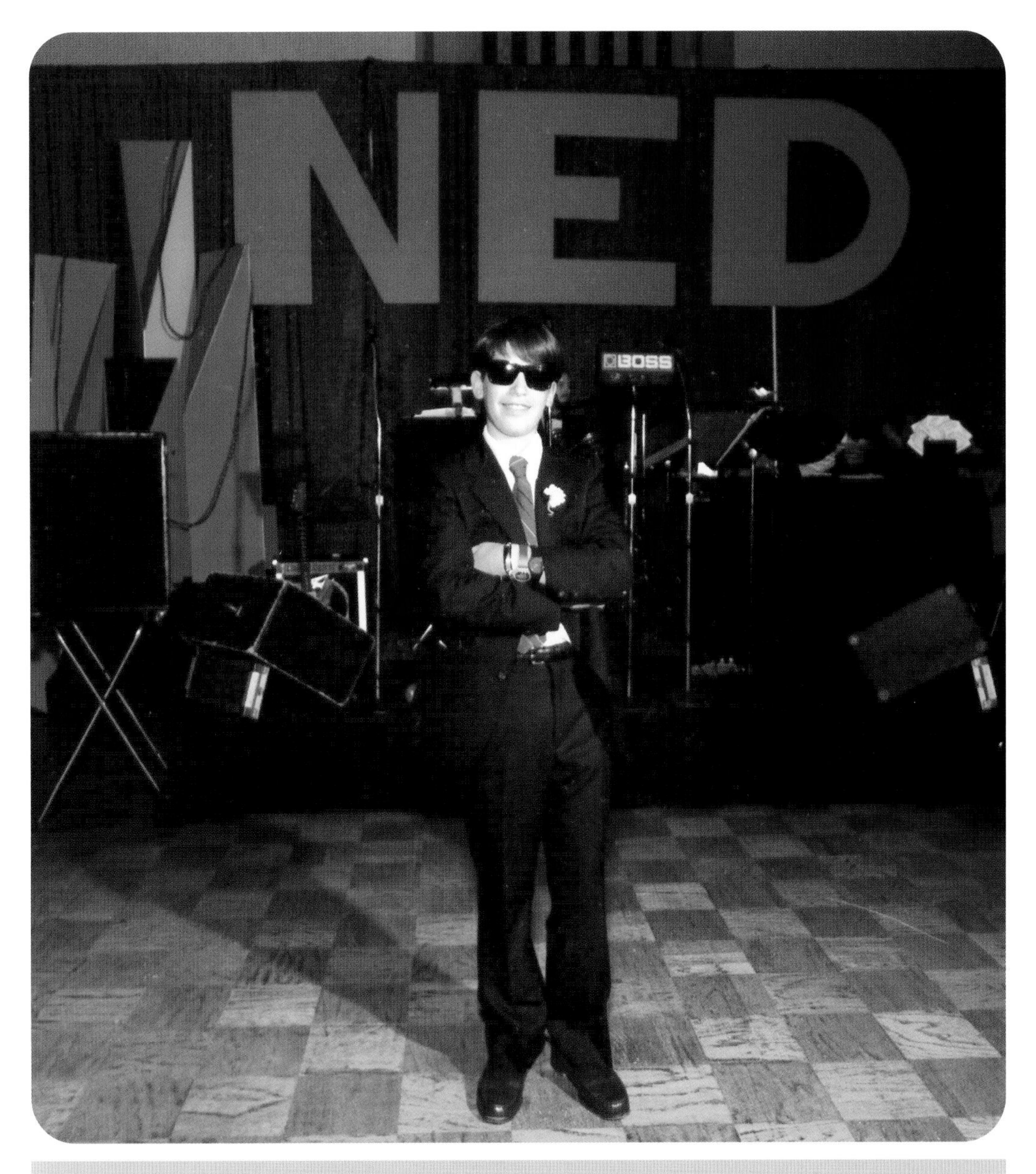

"My Bar Mitzvah was the culmination of my desperate quest to be accepted. I got not just one, but two pairs of Vuarnet sunglasses and walked around that whole week wearing one pair and carrying the other in a case on my belt."

Ned Lazarus
4.19.86
Washington, D.C.

"The nice thing about doing this with a twin was you only had to do half the work for the same amount of presents. The coolest was from my aunt who got me a digital watch with a built-in Space Invaders game. First of a kind in 1982."

David and Andi Shell
11.6.82
Columbus, Ohio

MBM

By NOAH TEPPERBERG

When I started to plan my Bar Mitzvah in June 1988, I really could not put a finger on what I wanted the theme to be, as there was no real "theme-able" topic that was representative of me or my hobbies. I was the fifth of five children. My older sister and two older brothers were all musicians, so it was pretty obvious what their theme would be. As a kid my hobby was chess, but as I got older, my interest dwindled and all I started to do was hang out with my "crew"—my closest group of friends. Rather than study chess or play after school in Washington Square Park, I would do what city kids did—hang around my neighborhood with my crew.

Two forces shaped me significantly at this time. First, I was a typical little brother who always looked up to his older brothers and wanted to be like them in every way possible, so obviously, a lot of my early interests were influenced by them. If they listened to reggae, I listened to reggae. If they liked to wear Ralph Lauren, so did I. Second, as someone who grew up in Manhattan and actually lived below 23rd Street, I had a lot of cultural exposure to things that were characteristic to living in this area of New York City. In the seventies and eighties, graffiti was one of those things.

A lot of my brothers' friends wrote graffiti—characters like Kostar, Tampa, Sher, and Cosm—so I would always pay attention to it and notice when new graffiti would appear on the walls around me or in the playgrounds I spent my afternoons hanging out in. Although I never wrote graffiti, many of my friends did. Most of the people I grew up with were identified by their graffiti names and "crews," which were usually identified by three letters that would follow graffiti writers' tags. The younger crews in the neighborhood always respected the older crews and would never write graffiti over theirs or copy their style.

So when it came to my Bar Mitzvah, my father took it upon himself to surprise me with a theme. He knew I always liked anything my older brothers liked, and more than anything, I always "wanted to be down with their crew," who were well respected in my neighborhood. So my dad got my brother to convince his friends to paint a "Noah"-themed mural to be used as the central decorative element at my Bar Mitzvah reception. This crew went by the name of New Crime Wave and were referred to throughout the city as NCW. They spent an evening on the rooftop of the building I grew up in at 14 Horatio Street with my dad and brother, spray-painting my name onto a hospital bedsheet. When I walked into the reception, they surprised me. There was the piece. It was colorful and blared out my name. It was cool and I was thrilled. This was the day I became recognized as an adult in my congregation. It was also the day my older brothers recognized me as part of their crew.

Matthew Issembert
6.6.92
Washington, D.C.

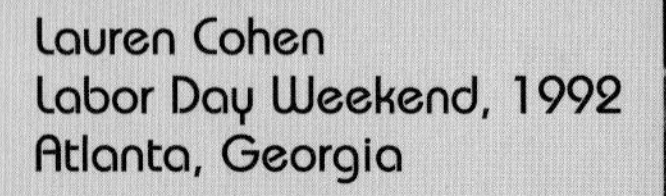

Lauren Cohen
Labor Day Weekend, 1992
Atlanta, Georgia

"Most people's themes are their hobbies. Apparently my mother thought mine was 'New York deli.' But it didn't matter . . . the DJ's name was bigger than mine. Most of the guests probably thought it was his Bat Mitzvah."

Eileen Quast
2.2.85
Stoney Creek Country Club
Columbus, Ohio

Violet Krumbein
8.4.90
Dallas, Texas

SIGN YOUR NAME

Sign your name across my heart
I want you to be my baby
—Terence Trent D'Arby

Why use a cheap guestbook when we all know it will only be consigned to a dusty shelf in the closet? Why not construct an elaborately designed sign-in board, force everyone to sign it, publicly attesting to your beauty, wisdom, and scholarly accomplishment, and then have the infinite pleasure of watching nature take its course as it rots away in your basement over the decades to come?

The sign-in board elevated the thirteen-year-old object of our attention to the place granted only to the most honorable ancestors in other noble religions. Their face at the center of a large board surrounded by a scattered representation of their most passionate pursuits like the telephone and Benetton shirts for the ladies. For the gents it was more often a guitar, a basketball, or even the greatest passion of any preteen in the suburbs: hardcore gangsta rap.

Josh Kun
8.18.84
Los Angeles, California

Bonnie Schwartz
6.13.92
Victor's Maywood Inn
Maywood, New Jersey

"My parents provided the list of interests for my sign-in board, hence the giant computer, disks, rocket ships, and comic books with references to sports at which I was mediocre at best. Like any other preteen white boy in the suburban Midwest, my greatest passion was hardcore gangsta rap. The caricaturist wasn't sure how to represent that, so instead of attempting a portrait of Flavor Flav, he settled for writing the word 'Rap!' in big letters."

Dan Powell
4.13.91
St. Louis, Missouri

Josh Speisman
11.25.89
Roslyn, New York

Matt Wood
3.15.86
The Palladium
New York, New York

Ali Waller
(pictured here at Disneyland)
11.9.91
The Regency Club
Los Angeles, California

PRINCESS OF ANAHEIM

By ALI WALLER

Sign-In boards should never be underestimated. With the exception of a balloon arc, they are the first decoration the guests see, and oftentimes the first display of the party's theme. Most normal girls fight with their mothers over the details of their themes every day for nine months prior to their Bat Mitzvah, but since I was already in trouble with Ali Rosen, a camp friend who had chosen a theme very similar to mine, my sign-in board became all-important.

Ali Rosen's theme was "Alison's Wonderland," based on the movie *Alice in Wonderland.* My theme was "Alison's Fantasyland," based on my personal ideas about what a fantasy-land might be like. Ali didn't believe this distinction, so in addition to the usual Bat Mitzvah stresses (picking invitations, theme, dress, table decorations, DJ, parting gifts, dinner, dessert; writing speeches for assorted friends and family members, learning to read Hebrew) I was preoccupied with making my Bat Mitzvah as different from Ali's as possible.

In retrospect I could have avoided this stress had I realized that since Ali and I lived on opposite sides of the country, none of the three friends we had in common would make it to both events anyway. Instead, I stressed.

Our party planner, Shelly Balloon (a legally changed name), suggested my sign-in board be a photograph of me, dressed in something fantastical, welcoming everyone into the party. I liked this idea, but felt it did not go far enough. When planning a Bat Mitzvah, the lines between elegant and gaudy become thinner as you cross from West LA into the Valley. I lived in West LA, home of everything considered chic and enviable. CW Designs, the shop where I had my dress made, was in Encino, a wasteland of pink nail polish and lip gloss. Although the drive down the 405 freeway was only twenty minutes, by taking it, we destroyed any chance I had of holding a simple, classy Bat Mitzvah.

The staff at CW adored me. They probably would have adored any Bat Mitzvah who chose to design her dress based on a Barbie ball gown. Unbelievably, in their ten-year history I happened to be the first. My dress was long and elegant. A full description of it would make excessive use of the following: *white, peach, lace, chiffon, flowers, floor-length,* and *really big bow in the back.* Because of the specificity of my order, I spent a lot of time at CW Designs, and when I needed to make the final decisions on my sign-in board I turned to the ladies there for help.

We spent hours discussing my possibilities. If I had been a makeshift Bat Mitzvah I would have used a baby picture where I was wearing some sort of tiara, or I would have taken pictures of myself dressed up and superimposed them in front of a cheesy picture of a castle. CW offered me a white fairy-like dress, but I wasn't pleased with the idea of a makeshift castle. Somehow my mother mulled over the scenarios for action, and mobilized all connections. A friend of the family called a friend of their family and soon I found myself on the way to Anaheim at seven o'clock in the morning, magic wand in hand, decked in a Tinkerbell-type dress, to be photographed in front of Disneyland's Magic Castle before the park opened. I would settle for no lame baby pictures, and I heard no complaints from Ali Rosen, who, incidentally, got sick last minute and couldn't make it to the party.

On the day of my Bat Mitzvah, the day I officially became a Jewish woman, I happily yet unknowingly epitomized the profile of a Jewish girl from Brentwood as I walked under a seafoam-and-peach balloon arc, past a photo of me in a fairy dress, hovering over Disneyland's Magic Castle, and into my own fantasyland dressed as a Jewish American Princess.

"Socks were a huge trend, but over-the-counter socks would not cut it for my mom. She had the designers at the dress shop create a pair to complement my dress. The socks were not allowed on my feet until after the candlelighting."

Abbey Orlofsky
11.9.91
Brae Burn Country Club
Purchase, New York

Barry Brown Studios
1995
Shea Stadium, Queens, New York

RED, RED WINE

You make me feel fine all of the time

Red, red wine

—UB40

After successfully navigating the stress of the "insurance claim waiting to happen" that is valet parking, and the flying elbows in line at the mothball-ridden coat check, the guests and family need to unwind. This is where the cocktail hour comes into play. Alongside an unhealthy fixation with country clubs and Ivy League schools, the cocktail hour is one of the important traditions American Jews have pilfered directly from their WASPy counterparts.

Never underestimate the twenty-five minutes known as the "cocktail hour." Keen observers of social dynamics understand this piece of social theater is where the seeds for the rest of the night are often sewn. Which aunt will successfully down enough white wine spritzers to use as an excuse when she ends up dry-humping one of the Teutonic hired dancers during the lambada? Will Grandma imbibe enough lite beer to cause her to temporarily suspend her jihad against her son-in-law, your father, "the no-good-nik who never was good enough for my daughter"? Will the vodka gimlets have the desired effect on the fleshy wallet you call "Dad" and allow him to momentarily forget how much the event is costing and enjoy himself, if just for a moment? All of these variables will be decided in the cocktail hour. Like the Olympic trials, some will walk away victorious while others are doomed to stumble off outside for some air, a quick smoke, and a belch.

Aaron Judah Bondaroff
3.17.90
New York, New York

Matt Weinberg
6.14.77
Long Island, New York

Adam Smith
11.5.83
Ridgeway Country Club
White Plains, New York

Michelle Shapiro
11.2.86
Battleground Country Club
Freehold, New Jersey

AND THE BAND PLAYED "KARMA CHAMELEON"

By JON WAGNER

For much of my life, I have displayed intensely chameleonesque characteristics. I have a strong desire to fit in with my surroundings, whatever and wherever they may be. You know the type—I'm barely out of passport control at Heathrow Airport before I have assumed a cockney accent fit for the cheekiest of chimney sweeps.

Back in seventh grade, with my first Bar Mitzvah imminent, I was an awkward gentile determined to belong. Once, there, I found myself in Washington Hebrew Congregation promising a Mrs. Rosen, whom I sat beside throughout the service, my bubbe's recipe for baked brisket—this even before we had left the temple. "My bubbe is such a cook," I'd say. "Can she cook." Doubtless she was pickling something that very moment. "Always pickling, my bubbe." How difficult to convey all this to Mrs. Rosen, for suddenly English had become my second language; my mother tongue was now an oft-neglected branch of Yiddish known only to me. An odd language to be sure, and one heavily dependent upon my ability to utter the word "shalom" for no apparent reason, yet with unusual frequency and without panache. A typical phrase might read as follows:

"Shalom, Mrs. Rosen. This my first Bar Mitzvah. Shalom, no?"

When accompanied by several errant, stuttered "mazel tovs," I was convinced of my fluency.

After the second airing of "Rock Lobster," gentle, gorgeous Mrs. Rosen asked me if perhaps I might be running a fever. I quickly retired to the bar for my eleventh Coke of that young evening of March 1987 on which Darren Rosen had become a man. Bobby Lamkin had been one for over a month; Josh Robbins practically seemed to be graying at the temples—he had been dating Stacy Lemonde for, like, nine days.

I remained, however, the boy puberty had forgotten. There would be no Bar Mitzvah of my own to reverse this fact—forever a schmuck without pubic hair wandering among the Chosen. Over the course of the next year and a half I would attend a dozen celebrations—certainly my most crowded social season to date. To this day, I still have six or seven satin yamulkes stowed in a drawer at my parents' home, each printed with name and date inside. I had glimpsed them before at school occasionally, in lockers or stuffed in the blazer pockets of those who had worn our school uniform to these Saturday affairs. Thirty or forty kids from an all-boy prep school in Bethesda, Maryland, would have donned anything to steal a glance of that forbidden garden of girls, one after the next dressed in the flowered cottons of Laura Ashley. These Bar and Bat Mitzvahs were a godsend; our escape from a campus that aspired to Spartan Greece. And I was agog. We all were. I would read the invitations three or four times a night. I would finger the raised print. I am fairly sure I had worried myself an ulcer over my choice of tie—I had all of three.

In April, Samuel Malasky appeared to rub the first hairs of a goatee while reading from the Torah. But they were only stitches—he had split his chin open the week before doing the Worm on the parquet floor of the JW Marriott. Everyone said he was lucky; it could have been much worse. Malcolm Malone broke up with Lisa Green during the first slow song of her Bat Mitzvah. I think we all heard her heart break. By May, Claire Marshall had made it clear to me she wanted to remain "just friends." So I spent the last minutes of Jeremy Kaplan's party with his great uncle Barry. His tie was undone; he'd pitted through his shirt while dancing. How I wish I might have said I traveled a great distance those hours in my seat at Washington Hebrew Congregation. How I felt the music of ancient language sound in my tiny chest. And the delight, the dewy delight of the turning of youth. Could I tell Uncle Barry that today? I am thirty-one years old, after all. May I tuck that *three* behind the fragile *one* and begin again? Is there a statute of limitations on becoming a man?

I remember Uncle Barry extending his enormous hand.

I said, "Shalom, my name is Jon. Jon without an *h.*"

He half-smiled and muttered, "Oy."

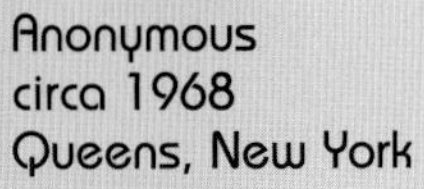
Anonymous
circa 1968
Queens, New York

Steven Klapow
7.4.82
Fontainebleau Caterers
Jericho, New York

Jennifer Koppell
4.23.83
Baton Rouge, Louisiana

TIME AFTER TIME

If you're lost you can look and you
will find me
Time after time
—Cyndi Lauper

A party is about to break out. But like any good bash, before it does, ritual—the act of marking both the holy day and the everyday—has to occur. In this case, the ritual is about giving Grandpa and Grandma three minutes max to light, pour, or slice anything they can get their hands on while a manic emcee sticks a static-ridden wireless mic in front of the old dears to catch their whispered blessings.

These three minutes of holy time are not without cost. Tipping a musty hat to the age-old traditions must be done with style. Give me three hundred color-coordinated velvet beanies with the Bar/Bat Mitzvah's name on it in Hebrew and in English on the inside, a wine goblet looted straight off King Arthur's Round Table, and make sure the challah is so large that it reflects our growing fortune, even if it makes Grandpa seem like he is wrestling an alligator in a swamp.

"Grandpa Ralph cut the Challah every time there was a Challah to cut."

Gary Benerofe
5.12.90
Bridgewaters
South Street Seaport
New York, New York

Samantha Benerofe
1988
Marriott Marquis
New York, New York

Craig Benerofe
11.22.86
The Manhattan Club
New York, New York

Lacey Schwartz
8.23.90
Seasons Restaurant
Woodstock, New York

THROUGH THE MEMORY GLASS DORKLY

By SCOTT GIMPLE

I have a terrible memory. I've forgotten much of my life, and the stuff that has stuck is piteously random. I remember lines from odd episodes of *Family Ties,* but I could only venture a guess as to the name of the first girl I ever kissed. The faces of most of my teachers are lost forever, but I can name all of the original VJs from MTV. I couldn't tell you what Torah portion I read at my Bar Mitzvah, but I can tell you that Adam Sank got up with the band and sang "(Ain't Nothin' Gonna) Break My Stride" at the reception.

So I guess it's not that odd I remember so much about the curious ritual of that time . . . the Bar Mitzvah memory glass.

Ah, the memory glass. A tumbler, wine flute, or on occasion, a crystal goblet, packed with mementos from the Bar Mitzvah, then filled with water and sealed with candle wax. A thing of beauty, but much like my mind, nearly useless for its central purpose of recollection. The impenetrable wax seal was always all-too penetrable, and within a week or two, the thing looked like the watery grave of the *Titanic:* bits of a glorious night would float in cloudy algae, giving off a haunted feeling, and making one come to wonder if the banquet hall had actually sunk that fateful eve.

Now, I can understand the urge to try to create an aide-mémoire to help capture each occasion, because this was a charged-up time. For many of us, it turned out to be the last time we felt truly alive. We were newly minted adults, with a stack of checks, the thumbs-up from rabbi, and either a *Miami Vice*–influenced suit or a smokin' dress from Bamburger's. What is hard to uncover are the elements that made the memory glass catch on as that aide-mémoire, because as anyone who actually tried to hold onto these decaying tokens could tell you, they soon had a bedroom that smelled like the swamps around the chemical plants off the New Jersey Turnpike.

What contributed to the institutionalization of the memory glass within the pantheon of prepubescent American popular culture was the intoxicating blend of exclusivity, theft, and fire that surrounded the act of its creation. While the critics were waiting impatiently upstairs, forming a conga line to Pac-Man Fever, the aesthetic decisions were being made far away from the reception, in the dark, with collage-happy members of the opposite sex taking the lead. There was a buzz that came from the mix of independence, puberty, pop music playing in the distance, an art project at hand, and close quarters.

So picture this, my own most powerful memory of the time. I am sitting on the floor in the darkened hallway of my empty Sunday School, a floor below the reception, across from three pretty girls with names like Liz, Amy, and Alison. One of them is in a green dress with white panty hose. We are each holding a candle, dripping wax onto the water inside the glass. "Come On Eileen" by Dexy's Midnight Runners is playing in the distance from upstairs. I look up and catch them all smiling, their Rachel Perry lip gloss reflecting the candlelight, all of them looking at me. There is potential. Things are beginning. Anything could happen.

"I wanted a Willy Wonka–themed party where everything would be edible — cotton candy machines, Sno-Cones, popcorn, and other treats. This is my aunt Terrie. She loves chocolate and spent most of her evening at the dessert table."

Bret Robins
2.13.89
Winding Hollow Country Club
Columbus, Ohio

HUNGRY LIKE THE WOLF

Mouth is alive, all running inside

And I'm hungry like the wolf.

—Duran Duran

After seeing their Holy Temple destroyed for a second time in A.D. 70, the Jewish people shrewdly started to worship at an altogether different kind of sacred altar . . . the buffet table. Like a herd of hungry bison roaming the plains for sweet, fresh grass on which to graze, celebrants hit the finger food hard. And they expected to be satiated. The buffet was a feeding frenzy in which a medium-sized smoked fish (with the Bar Mitzvah boy's name spelled on it in olives and pimentos) would be stripped to the bone in a time span that would make the most vicious shoal of piranha reach for the Pepto-Bismol.

The Jewish people have made many contributions to the modern world. The theory of relativity and the Hollywood studio system may come to mind. Arguably, our obsessive pursuit of the perfect two-bite pig in a blanket will have the most longevity. To mark this fact, the fleet-of-foot photographer would whisk the Bar or Bat Mitzvah around every part of the buffet table as if they were Stations of the Cross. Hence we are gifted with these shots of mildly mortified youths at the carving station, serving popcorn, and reluctantly taste-testing the consistency of toffee apples.

"This is the quintessential photo of my father. He was never happier than when serving copious amounts of well-done meat to family and friends."

Julie Hermelin
9.5.80
Southfield, Michigan

Elissa Stein
6.18.77
Woodbury, New York

"This is completely posed. Even at thirteen, I would not have eaten a Goldenberg Peanut Chew or a candy apple."

Steven Klapow
7.4.82
Fontainbleau Caterers
Jericho, New York

"I grew up a triple outsider — fat, Jewish, and gay in Flint, Michigan. I have never felt more fat, Jewish, or gay than at my Bar Mitzvah. Fat? The vest of my olive sharkskin suit had to be sacrificed for my pants. Jewish? My uncle, the rabbi, wouldn't let me learn my haftarah from a recording. Gay? Who do you think planned the party? Fortunately, I moved to Los Angeles later in life where being fat, Jewish, and gay were three rungs on the ladder of success."

Howard Bragman
3.1.69
Flint, Michigan

Julie Hermelin
9.5.80
Southfield, Michigan

TABLES TURNING

Help yourself to another bite
Everything will be alright
—Modern English

The table shot marked a turning point in the event. It was the last time you saw the Bar Mitzvah boy unblemished—his shirt remotely tucked in, without any of the mysterious stains that were soon to colonize his pants. The table shot also captured the Bar or Bat Mitzvah as they wanted to be perceived. They controlled the table plan, and could use that power to seat themselves between the hottest girls and the coolest guys, while banishing their real friends to Siberia or at least to the outer fringes of the tent.

Whether it is the wide-angle shot of Table Number One that at first glance looks like an oil painting of the Last Supper, the parents' best friends soon to be divorced, or a candid capturing the older sister with the boyfriend she demanded be treated like family and then dumped the next week, the table shot pays homage to the casts of thousands who turned the average Bar Mitzvah into the likes of a Presidential Inauguration, minus the president, and the inauguration.

Anonymous
circa 1968
Queens, New York

"Why I was snapping my fingers remains a mystery to this day. I suspect I was simply commanded to do so by the photographer."

Mark Melnick
6.5.71
Aperion Manor, Kings Highway
Brooklyn, New York

Ira Kane
1963
The Concourse Hotel
The Bronx, New York

Michelle Shapiro
11.2.86
Battleground Country Club
Freehold, New Jersey

David Measer
5.5.84
Chasen's Restaurant
Hollywood, California

WWJD?

By AMBER BONADIO

In seventh grade, a new social phenomenon appeared out of nowhere—the Bar Mitzvah party. As a non-Jew, I had some vague understanding that the ceremony symbolized the passing into adulthood. I knew that my closest Jewish friends had been forced to endure Friday night temple services and Saturday one-on-one tutoring with their rabbi. But other than that, the Bar and Bat Mitzvah was basically an opportunity for a huge party, conveniently timed with our first forays into drinking excessive amounts of alcohol and making out.

The very first one we went to set the standard for every one of my Jewish friends who had the ceremony fast approaching in their own immediate futures. From a kid's perspective you were luckier to have yours later in the year, because the parties became incrementally over the top. Obviously, for their parents who had to finance our hedonism, the opposite was probably true.

By the end of seventh grade, I had probably attended no less than a dozen ceremonies and parties. To this day I have a specific part of the Torah service memorized. Please note, I was somewhat of an expert among the novice gentile pubescent teens getting dropped off at temple every other Friday night. I had attended a temple once before for a plain old regular Friday night service with some of my Jewish friends. (Side note: at the end of the service, I was amazed to discover they served food and wine in their little reception area, which I thought was a wonderful idea that Catholics should adopt to prevent people from sneaking out after communion. I also remember leaning over to get something and a candle on the table ignited the 2.5 pounds of hair spray in my hair and some kindly Jewish mother had to pound out the flames on my head.)

Receiving an invite to a "cool" kid's Bar Mitzvah was an indication of your social standing. To be cut from the guest list was socially humiliating, especially for a non-Jew, as teen members of the same temple were a guaranteed invite. Maybe I was a wannabe Jew, or a Bar Mitzvah groupie. Who knows what was deemed cool for a thirteen-year-old in America in 1989, but in my town, the number of Bar Mitzvahs you attended were like proverbial notches in the belt.

From the moment the invitation came, the next issue was what you would wear. I quickly learned there was the ceremony on Friday night (more often than not, I raided my mother's closet), the Saturday afternoon small family get-together (if you were really close to the honoree), and then the blowout Saturday night party.

These parties were like a night of debauchery lived PG-13 style, like mini-weddings for thirteen-year-olds. Just a year later in eighth grade, the equivalent of the Bar Mitzvah pops up in the Catholic faith. Confirmation. For some reason, though, there are no crazy parties, and no huge receptions. I don't even remember any guest list, catered food, or any sneaking off for cigarettes. My confirmation consisted of two dozen relatives coming over for brunch.

Now, reflecting back from a more mature angle, I'm pretty happy that our town and the people in it were so open. I think I grew up with a better understanding of Judaism than most Italian-Catholic kids. I think for a lot of Christians, Judaism remains a mysterious and cryptic religion with specific ceremonies, rules, and customs that are so different from our own. I have some pretty kick-ass pictures documenting my interactions with this cryptic religion: big hair, horrible dresses, vests (I was very partial to vests that year), and bad dance moves, as evidenced in the dozen videos I still own from those Bar Mitzvahs. These events were the Holy Grail of our social activities.

Richard Shell
10.4.80
Columbus, Ohio

Doug Herzog
6.3.72
Paterson, New Jersey

Gary Benerofe
5.12.90
Bridgewaters
South Street Seaport
New York, New York

EBONY AND IVORY

Ebony and ivory
live together in perfect harmony
—Paul McCartney and Stevie Wonder

If ever proof was needed to illustrate that the school busing experiments of the early seventies were not everything the social scientists promised they would be, the Bar Mitzvah party may be it. This was an era in which mixed marriages increased and previously impermeable ethnic boundaries became porous. But while there seemed to be as many Irish and Italians as Jews at Bar and Bat Mitzvahs in this period, there only ever seemed to be one black kid at the party, just like there was always only one white guy on every episode of *Showtime at the Apollo.*

This section pays tribute to those who faced the heavy burden of being the sole representative of an entire race. Watch them cut the cake, mug it up with their buddies, and ham it up on stage with the professional dancer bedecked from head to toe in scuba gear.

THE LONELIEST BLACK KID

By JORDAN CARLOS

And now the Torah portion's been read,
"Baruch aloha henu" has been said,
Time once again for after-party fun,
It's little Joshy Goldberg's moment in the sun,
But I take pause for maybe just a minute,
To wonder how I got here
And ponder my place in it,
For I am the onliest,
I am the loneliest,
Black kid at the Bar Mitzvah,
My rayon tie is tied so tight,
"More than words," pumps through the air,
But still I wonder as I slow dance,
What am I doing here?
Oh to be the token,

When "Motown/Philly" is requested,
You're asked to dance the running man,
By the brace-faced and flat-chested,

And as I look back upon simpler days,
On the Mr. Bigs and LL Cool Js,
To the halcyon year that was the sixth grade,
When I tried to fit a yarmulke on a high-top fade,
My eyes begin to twinkle,
And I remember with delight,
At being Black at the Bar Mitzvah
When all the other kids were white.

David and Jono Kohan
4.16.77
Los Angeles, California

Jim Cone
10.13.79
Wayne, New Jersey

GIRLS ON FILM

See them walking hand in hand across the bridge at midnight,
Heads turning as the lights flashing out it's so bright
—Duran Duran

The journey into adulthood posed some of the most powerful existential questions a human can be forced to consider. Especially for a special young lady whose body was literally changing every day. Would you dress like the girl you were or the woman you so badly wanted to be? Would you wear makeup or would your beauty shine through au naturel? Would that dress be strapless, or even backless? Were the number of ruffles appropriately in ratio with the height of the bangs you were sporting? Were your shoes flat or would you take the plunge and wear heels? Would those shoes be ditched and replaced with a pair of socks after the candlelighting? Against the vicious backdrop of power plays and changing alliances of the Bat Mitzvah circuit, would your Best Friend Forever still be speaking to you by the end of the evening?

Unfortunately, the answers to most of these questions were not in your hands. They were partially in your mother's—it was she who would give you permission to have your braces removed by the orthodontist the week before the Bat Mitzvah and slapped back in the week after. But the ultimate determinant was the stage your body was at and whether you had little boobs, no hips, and an artfully padded bra, or were fully developed and ready to thrust those brand-new breasts in the face of the nearest suitor, even if he was just five feet tall.

Elissa Bowes
10.13.90
The Waterfall Room, The Sheraton
Wayne, New Jersey

JENNIFER GREY'S NOSE

By JESSI KLEIN

I have one really clear memory of watching my brother sitting next to the rabbi on his little twin bed with the *Star Wars* sheets, the two of them pouring over his Torah portion, speaking in low and unintelligible tones. I was nine years old at the time, and from my vague understanding of what he was being asked to do, I found the task of preparing for his Bar Mitzvah staggeringly frightening. The rabbi was a large and intimidating man whose black overcoat and hat made him appear about five times larger than he probably was. My brother was of course twelve, but next to this husky man with the long beard he looked even younger. In the months leading up to the ceremony, I kept thinking, as I have often in my life, how glad I was not to be my brother, and how relieved I was not to be saddled with what I thought of as an endlessly unpleasant list of male responsibilities, which at the time, in my innocence, was topped by exclusive obligations to work nine to five and occasionally punch bullies.

When I turned twelve, I was beginning a battle with an awkward phase that had come over me with the intensity of a "shock and awe" campaign, including the full arsenal of glasses, braces, and inappropriate height. The notion of a Bat Mitzvah was a snarled knot of uncomfortable propositions, threading together public speaking,

Hebrew learning, and dress wearing, all of which seemed either dreadfully difficult, hugely embarrassing, or both. So it was with great relief when my father finally got around to letting me know that in his opinion, Bat Mitzvahs were a relatively newfangled Jewish invention that were not considered essential, and if I didn't want one, I did not have to have one. I've since fact-checked, and it turns out my father was (uncharacteristically) wrong, and Jewish women have been getting Bat Mitzvahed since the fifteenth century. I (very characteristically) was more than happy to get out of extra work and passed on the whole shebang.

But sixteen years later, as I've lived through the latter half of my twenties, I've often paused to wonder if I have yet "become a woman." Unlike Britney Spears, these pauses have not inspired me to write a tinny *Billboard*-topping pop song, but I don't think that makes the wondering any less valid. I remember looking at my hopelessly gawky, baby-faced brother in his Bar Mitzvah suit and thinking how ridiculous it was that someone so clearly a child would be getting the official nod of adulthood from the letter of Jewish law. But in those moments when, at age twenty-eight, I still find myself struggling to emote the emotional authority of adulthood, I begin to think that perhaps one of the greater values of the ceremony might have been in simply walking through a gateway that an entire community has agreed to view as your official entry to emotional and sexual maturity, regardless of the absence of breasts or presence of a night brace.

But since I haven't had a Bat Mitzvah, I've started looking back on my adolescence for other tent-pole growth experiences that ring familiar with a large enough sector of the contemporary Jewish community to in some way amount to a kind of Bat Mitzvah GED, an accumulation of catch-as-catch-can transformative experiences that have earned me enough credits to get into the only sorority I have ever wanted to join, that exclusive, beautiful sisterhood of full-fledged Jewish women.

Maybe because it's the decade when I turned thirteen, but to me, the pop culture of the eighties had an identity as characteristically schizophrenic as the average adolescent's. By turns slutty (Tiffany) and innocent (Debbie Gibson), in retrospect, those ten years now seem to me to perfectly embody the aspirations of the teenager, a time when ambition to separate yourself from what's come before you leads you to sexual boundary pushing and ambitious rebellion that can ultimately cause both extreme embarrassment and extreme growth. Weathering those years myself, I definitely tasted both, and looking back, I've identified three milestones in my adolescence that I think were overlaps with popular enough milestones in the decade's teenagerdom that I hope my female peers will give me the nod of recognition until I finally make it up and get the real deal Bat Mitzvah—something I still sincerely hope to do. Whether these milestones are in any way uniquely Jewish, I can't say for sure, but I think there's a case to be made for each one.

#3—I had my first "wet dream" the night after seeing "Dirty Dancing"

As unforgettably great a movie as this is, the night after I saw it for the first time was even more so. I was twelve years old, and I went to the movie with my best friend, Molly. We sat in the theater together, silent the way you're supposed to be in a theater but even more silent, because for the duration of the film we were barely breathing. The feeling we had watching that movie was as close as either of us had come to knowing what sex would be like. Who could imagine anything hotter than having Patrick Swayze squint upon your flat but heaving bosom with his beady eyes as he pressed you into his pro-dancer thighs? Who could imagine a more romantic cherry-popping than on a crappy futon in a Catskills bungalow to the tune of "Cry to Me"? And then there was Jennifer Grey's original, beautiful Jewish schnoz, emerging from the screen sloped but firm like one of the stamen in a Georgia O'Keeffe painting, both phallic and feminine all at once. That night I went to sleep desperately trying to keep every moment of that dirty-dance opening montage in my head, the vibrations of Ronnie Spector's weird, viscose voice in my ears. I was forcibly awakened by my own body as I found myself having an insanely intense first ever big-O. I've taken an informal poll, and the results are unanimous—3 out of 3 of my closest friends had this same experience. Yes, all three are shiksas, but I believe it was the vulnerability and innocence of Jennifer's Jew-y, pre-nose-job honker next to Patrick's buffitude that made this movie so transcendently hot.

#2—My friends and I practiced kissing on a George Michael door poster

The year was 1989, and my friend Orange (yes, that's her name, and of course she was Jewish—in my experience, only Jewish hippie parents really went the extra mile with the weird names) was turning fourteen. My friends and I went to PosterMat on 8th Street to get her the gift that, yes, she had asked for, but only as a formality; she knew we knew what she wanted—because she wanted what we all wanted: a life-size door poster of George Michael. In our minds, George was the ultimate sex symbol, and having a crush on such a bad boy, such a pillar of fiery, untamed heterosexuality, made us sexy too. When the poster was unrolled at the slumber party, it immediately went up on the door, where flat George was treated to an evening of tweenage girls leaving pink frost lipstick kisses all over his mouth, neck, and—oh yes—crotch. That's right. I said it.

Now, yes, *Faith* was a multiplatinum album and I'm sure girls of all creeds did blow-job batting practice on some kind of George effigy. But if *Will & Grace* has taught us anything, and I believe it has, it's that accidentally falling in love with a gay man is as essential a rite of passage to a Jewish girl as communion wafers are to our Catholic friends. George was the classic combination of libido and sensitivity that has lured Jewish women into doomed relationships for ages; he insisted he wanted our sex with thrilling urgency, but would a real dog have the tenderness to write "explore monogamy" in lipstick on his girlfriend's thigh? No, a dog wouldn't; but a straight man probably wouldn't either. We repressed that thought and decided such a sentiment showed a real capacity for love. It's also important to note that during the *Faith* period, if his videos were any indication, George seemed to have a real penchant for Asian girls, which only ignited our lust further with the fuel of familiar jealousy.

#1—Tuberculosis cast a shadow over my first date

What's a more important milestone in a young girl's journey to womanhood than her first kiss? At fourteen, all of my friends had been kissed by someone, or multiple someones. Yes, many of these guys had mullets, but that didn't matter. The relay race to slutville had left me the sole holder of the unkissable baton, and I was desperate to pass it off. Fourteen was unacceptably old to never have been kissed, but I was a bookish, nerdy chick before that was fashionable, and I just wasn't having any luck. I was really into Kafka and *The Metamorphosis,* not a hot topic for dudes. My fortune seemed to change one night when I went out with Molly and her boyfriend, Steve, a nice enough guy who had gone a few inches past mullet and now had enough length to rock-glam-band hair. Steve brought along his friend Dave, who as a Jersey-based college freshman had attained a car. I sat shotgun while Molly and Steve made out in the back. Dave and I didn't have much to say to each other that night, primarily because I was in such disbelief at his full commitment to a rat tail that I couldn't really form words.

The next morning Molly informed me of the "good news" that Dave had a crush on me and wanted my number. The prospect of anyone liking me enough to kiss me seemed to warrant overlooking the rat tail—I mean, he would most likely kiss me with the side of his head that did not have the rat tail on it anyway. He called and we made a plan to go see *Bird on a Wire,* starring Goldie Hawn and Mel Gibson, two people who would go on to spawn separate vessels of evil: Goldie's in the form of Kate Hudson, Mel's in his flick *The Passion.* I didn't care what we saw, as long as we kissed.

It's a tale as old as TV ads—the day of the big date, a pimple, a period, or some other physical malady comes along to spoil the whole thing. But those are wholesome, run-of-the-mill annoyances compared to my case, in which the buzzkill came in the form of a tuberculosis scare. My father was a probation officer who often had to visit "clients" at Rikers, a notorious hot zone for the disease. An hour before I was to leave, as I was doing a last fitting of my bowler-hat-and-vest date outfit (I took my fashion cues from *Pretty in Pink*'s Duckie), my father came home from work looking gloomy. He informed us that there was the possibility he had TB and we would all have to be tested. When he saw I had my bowler on he knew it was a special occasion, and I confessed that I was an hour away from my first date. We then endured one of the most awkward moments in the history of our relationship as he instructed me, painfully, "No kissing." I was in such a state of shock that when I met up with Dave, all I said was, "I just found out I might have tuberculosis so I can't kiss you." To say that the date was the worst date of all time would be a severe understatement.

TB may have felled my personal favorite Jewish literary hero, Franz Kafka. But we found out I didn't have TB, and neither did my dad. It was an ironic double blessing—thanks to God, of course, that we were not sick—but thanks also to the grim shadow of the disease for saving me from taking my first kiss from Rat Tail. That awkward honor went a year later to a very nice young man who, much more appropriate to what I could handle at the time, was a clean-cut freshman at Brandeis.

"There was no second base for me. Although I would have loved it. Puberty had a different plan for me. I would have to wait a long time before a boy was to ever touch my peanuts. That was the name my breasts were given by my circle of girlfriends."

Stacy Marcus (center row, far right)
5.26.90
Wayne, New Jersey

"Every Bar Mitzvah ended with a rendition of 'That's What Friends Are For.' We would gather in a huge circle, and sing as if it were around the fire on the last night of camp, even though we knew we would all see each other the next weekend, to do the same exact thing." —Elissa Bowes

Alan Bowes
2.14.87
The Pool Room, The Sheraton
Wayne, New Jersey

WILD BOYS

Wild boys never close your eyes,
Wild boys always shine
—Duran Duran

The one part of the evening that routinely vexed even the most experienced of Bar Mitzvah photographers was the boys' group shot. The challenge of herding together a dozen mouthy varmints whose Ritalin was wearing off meant that this was most often orchestrated at lightning speed, with the photographer blithely ignorant of the social dynamics at play. For one moment in time, the mathlete, the bully, the Dungeons & Dragons aficionado, the stoner, and the jock would be crushed together in a straight line, or occasionally in a human pyramid. It is clear from each shot just who will be getting lucky later in the night and who will be left to go home and make out tenderly with their pillow.

These images are a collection of raging hormones frozen in time. Like a scientific chart detailing Darwin's theory of evolution, the boys line up in their different states of pubescent progression. Each shot appears to be a casting call for *Lord of the Flies,* with the strong dominating the center, the weak forced to the fringes, and everyone pleading for the photographer's attention. The camera would inevitably be drawn to the blondest of hair and the bluest of eye. The lotharios in training, named Chad, Clay, or Oliver, were most often at the peak of their sexual and social existence. Their confidence and poise could unnerve even the most happily of married men at the affair. The photographer would count to three and everyone would desperately attempt to capture the poise of one of their heroes—Rocky, Arnold Schwarzenegger, the "Boz," Flavor Flav, or Latke from *Taxi.* Despite their best efforts, the collective effect was inevitably one of a gay boys' choir.

"The Robutler was wheeled out during the cocktail hour in front of my house. He was fairly new to the party-planning universe and there was a great sense of mystery as to how he was controlled. Was there a 'little person' in that tin can, or was there someone perched up in a tree with a remote control? That, I suppose, was the wonder of the Robutler."

David Javitch
5.27.89
Harrison, New York

THE JOY[STICK] OF MANHOOD

BY DAVID WAIN

My Bar Mitzvah (June 12, 1982, Shaker Heights, Ohio) was two months shy of my thirteenth birthday, and about a year shy of my first kiss. At this point all my friends were boys, so unlike some of my more advanced stud-guy friends, my big celebration was an all-boys affair.

And just to make sure no girls would accidentally stop by, the party took place in my garage, which was filled with rented coin-operated video games—all set on free-play. This was during that summer when video games had reached a critical mass, especially with thirteen-year-old boys. This was truly heaven on earth.

After the morning ceremony and a brief lunch to appease the grown-ups, I ripped off my suit (which my best friend and I bought together for our Bar Mitzvahs, knowing each of us would wear it once) and made a beeline for the oasis of unlimited Donkey Kong, Frogger, and Ms. Pac-Man, waiting to be played, no quarters needed. Myself and twenty other boys spent a euphoric day and night moving joysticks and pressing buttons, taking periodic breaks for swimming and fried chicken.

The consoles stayed in the garage for a few days, and my skills on each game improved dramatically. To this day I can out-Frogger or out-Donkey anyone who dares to challenge me.

And then there's Ms. Pac-Man. The pièce de résistance.

Because, when the truck came and picked up all the other games, the Ms. Pac-Man was moved into our basement, where it stayed, for *three weeks,* as a surprise present. Kill me now, why don't you? So I spent that whole three weeks sitting in the dark basement, playing lots and lots of Ms. Pac-Man. While I took brief sleep breaks at night to appease my parents, I mostly sat there, deftly controlling that beautiful yellow pie-chart-shaped thingy with the bow in her hair. By the time three weeks were up I was so good it was scary. I found levels the game didn't know it had. But it came at a price. I had spent so much time sitting, leaning on my left elbow as I played, that I lost all feeling on the side of my left arm, rendering me unable to wail on the guitar (also lack of ability or talent). It took several trips to the neurologist and a summer of wearing an elbow pad before the feeling returned.

But it was all worth it because today, I can go into any fancy-ass video game room, walk past all the Virtua Fighter games and find that neglected Ms. Pac-Man sitting in the corner. And when the youngsters witness my prowess with the joystick, when they see just how many dots I can eat, they bow down before me, the Old Master. Plus I chanted my haftarah from memory.

Doug Herzog
6.3.72
Paterson, New Jersey

"The guy in the center, Chad, was the most wanted man at all the Bar / Bat Mitzvahs. He was not even Jewish. I had a crush on four of the ten guys shown in the picture."

Debbie Shell
5.16.87
Columbus, Ohio

OLD SCHOOL

This Bar Mitzvah is so perfectly old school, it deserves its own book. What could be a more appropriate place for a boy to have his day of days than Coney Island, one of the original Jewish entertainment shrines? This album tells the story of Ruslan and his family, originally from Odessa, transplanted to New York, and a perfect symbol of the porous boundaries of the modern American community. Take a Russian mother and an Italian-American stepfather, put them in a Russian banquet hall for a celebration of manhood, and capture the whole event with a photographer who never met a double exposure he did not love.

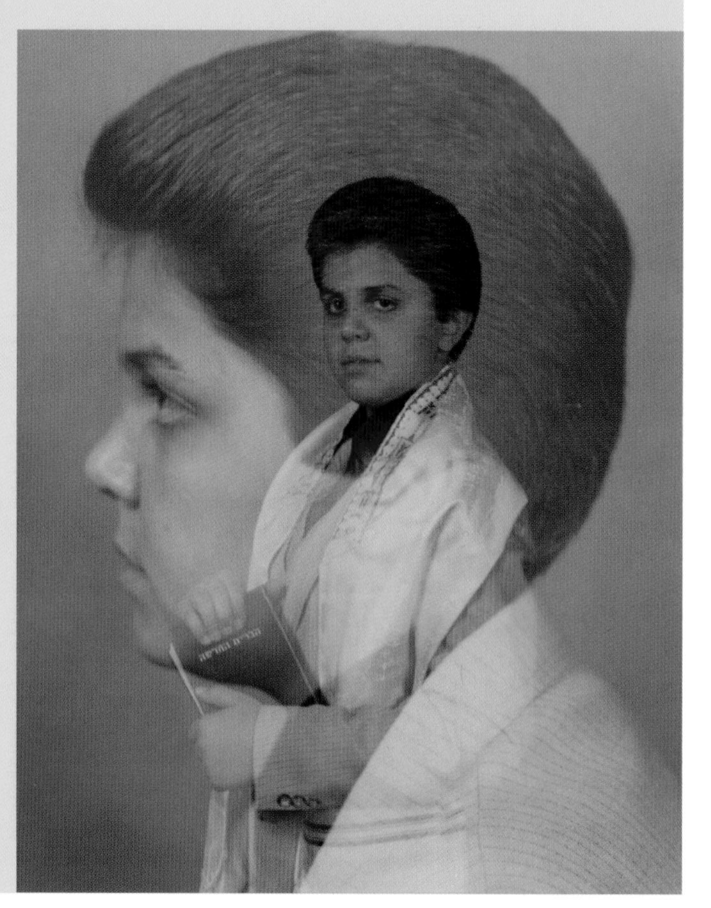

Ruslan Karablin
8.14.82
Coney Island, New York

"We had the party at Lisa Terrace in Canarsie. It was a Russian party hall with cabaret and dancing. They had showgirls — not strip-tease but Vegas-style dancers with feathers. The party was Russians and Italians getting drunk together. When they called my godmother up they played the theme to The Godfather. *She wore a dress to go with it. It was mostly family who came — but there were some characters. You'd pat them on the back and you didn't know if it was a wallet back there or something else."*

My Bar Mitzvah
Russell
August 14, 1982

Robert Cohen
6.27.82
Brooklyn, New York

LADY IN RED

I've never seen you looking so lovely as you did tonight
I've never seen you shine so bright
—Chris de Burgh

For the Bat Mitzvah girl, decisions to be made around issues of style were a crucial component of the rite of passage. Once you had persuaded your mother to forgo her attempts to outshine you in her little number, there was the excruciating ritual of countless visits to boutiques with names like Today's Teen to piece together the arsenal of outfits necessary for the synagogue service, the luncheon, cocktails, and the disco itself. These getups had to be individually dazzling yet sufficiently flexible to be repurposed with an array of accessories for the rest of the Bar Mitzvah season. While the affluent were able to acquire more dresses than parties, most were forced to rotate a select few. Your peers were cruel so you quickly learned to remember exactly what you wore to which event.

The Bar/Bat Mitzvah circuit was a chance for all to model the very latest in haute couture. To our modern eye, most garments look as if they had spent very little time on the catwalks of Paris and Milan before ending up on the rack at Loehmann's. But this is a gallery of Bar/Bat Mitzvah fashion evergreens that never go out of style—shoulder pads, asymmetrical hemlines, gaping cleavages, and the calm, safe waters of ruffles, ruffles, and more ruffles.

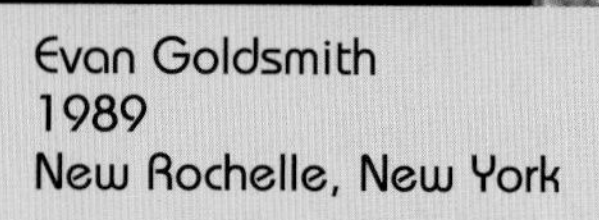

Evan Goldsmith
1989
New Rochelle, New York

Doug Herzog
6.3.72
Paterson, New Jersey

Sarra Cooper
5.18.91
Middle Bay Country Club
Oceanside, New York

Scott Jacoby
10.31.84
Westchester, New York

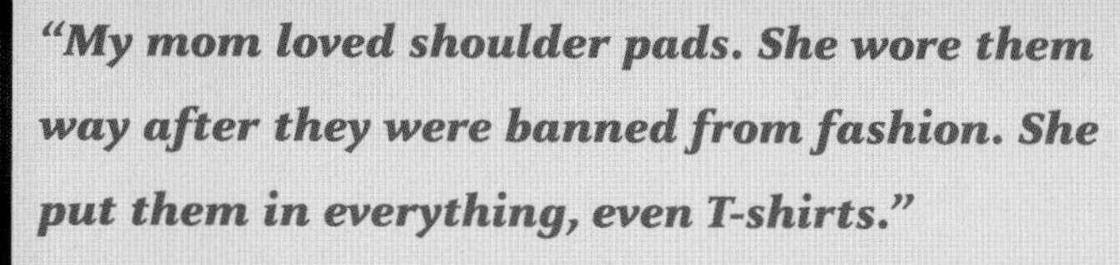

"My mom loved shoulder pads. She wore them way after they were banned from fashion. She put them in everything, even T-shirts."

Stacy Marcus
5.26.90
Wayne, New Jersey

Michael Larsen
5.27.73
Regency House
Jamaica, Queens, New York

ETERNAL FLAME

Do you feel my heart beating,
do you understand?
—The Bangles

Candlelighting was a tricky part of the proceedings. By now the guests were fed, socially lubricated, and ready to scuff the soles of their shoes on the dance floor for a couple of tunes before driving home drunk. Candlelighting was the last obligatory hurdle before this could occur and so was often an excruciating ritual in which the total giddiness of the honoree was matched only by widespread disgruntled boredom among those doomed to spectate.

But as these images suggest, the ceremony should be viewed as a piece of intriguing social commentary. Exactly which friends and family were herded up to offer rote speeches or to deliver in-jokes? Were only school friends called up or were camp friends honored as well? Together or separately? Did you have the confidence to call up friends of the opposite sex? And if so, did you seal the deal with a kiss? In the words of one eighties' Bar Mitzvah boy, "The highlight of my affair was getting a girl called Jackie to come up and kiss me, on the lips no less. She was the most popular girl in my grade, primarily because she had the largest breasts. It instantly conveyed a certain status on me, even though it was essentially coerced. Poor Jackie, she was invited up by 90 percent of the boys in my class."

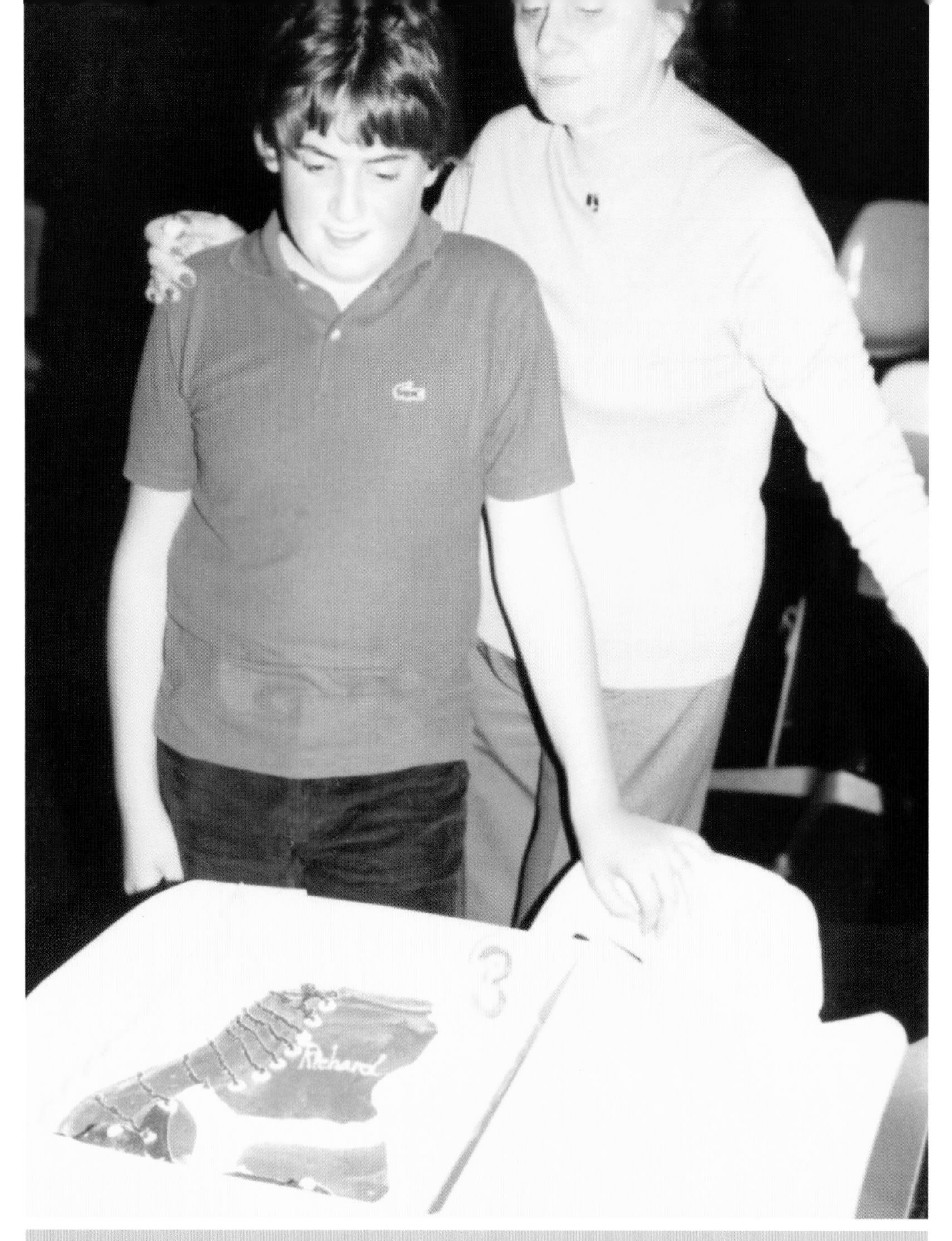

"I was kind of at an awkward stage in my life so it was great to be the center of attention and to feel like I was in the 'popular' group, if only for an hour or two. I appreciate it all as I look back but I wish I did not have to buy my clothes in the husky department."

Richard Shell
10.4.80
Columbus, Ohio

THE TRAVESTY OF OLD BRIDGE NEW JERSEY

By JOEL STEIN

For seven years I was pretty satisfied with the greatest day of my life: I had spoken at length in a language I didn't understand one word of and was lifted in a chair in a moment of triumph usually reserved for dead Iranian leaders. I had cool gray suede yamulkes with all three of my names written inside, a baseball centerpiece made of 100 percent genuine Styrofoam, a memory glass that didn't contain any biodegradable materials, and a rousing game of Coke and Pepsi in which Bizzy's crinoline skirt flew up every time she ran to sit on Heather's knee. 7-Up indeed.

Then my parents threw my sister Lisa's Bat Mitzvah. Sure, my parents were richer by then. And feeling guilty for recently separating. And my sister is a lot more demanding than I am. But that does not justify the Travesty of Old Bridge New Jersey.

The first thing I saw upon walking into my sister's Bat Mitzvah at the Grand Marquis in Manhattan were the words "Lisa on Broadway" spelled out in lightbulbs in a ten-foot-by-twenty-foot sign that the producers of *Mamma Mia!* would be jealous of. There was a guy with a cotton candy stand, an airbrush artist making customized T-shirts, an ice-cream sundae bar, a band with enough Glo-sticks to spell out "Lisa on Broadway" yet again, and a videographer documenting this with footage that, were my father the CEO of a large corporation, would have gotten him thrown in jail. Members of the Soprano family would comment that the party was a little tacky. Seated in the corner at what I'm pretty sure was not accidentally the "Les Misérable Table," all I could picture was my Bar Mitzvah, in the wood-paneled back of our suburban temple, decorated only with a row of colored balloons tied at the ends to vaguely denote the shape of a rainbow. My sister had a gay county fair fantasia, while I had that Iowan insurance agent retirement party from the beginning of *About Schmidt.*

A less secure man would have assumed that his parents loved his sister more than him. Not me. I just assume they give her more because she's a whiner. I don't know how, twenty years after my Bar Mitzvah, I expect them to even the score, but I do know it should involve a buttload of cotton candy.

Perhaps dredging all this up this past Mother's Day in the hospital room where my eighty-eight-year-old grandmother was hooked up to an IV unit wasn't the best time. But true injustice treats the world as its courtroom. Plus, it was crazy boring in there.

I barely started questioning my mother about the Travesty of Old Bridge New Jersey when she became defensive. "I thought your Bar Mitzvah was incredibly warm in the temple. It's where it should be," said my mother, a woman who has not been to a temple since my Bar Mitzvah. Then, in a moment of desperation, she added, "You had a pasta station." Yes, Mom, it was an Olive Garden good time.

When I reminded her of the party favors we gave out to my thirteen-year-old friends—real mini-clipboards with real pads of paper and real pencils—she fell silent. "We gave out pads?" she asked.

At this point in the conversation, my sister called me an "asshole" and explained that the very logical rationale for her having a nicer Bat Mitzvah was "probably because I wanted it." Plus, she explained, she had to keep up with her friends who were having much nicer events than mine ever had. "A lot of my friends were really wealthy," she explained. "Unlike you, I was in private school." I was starting to see just how far this thing goes.

I like to think my Bar Mitzvah toughened me up for the experiences I would face throughout the rest of my life, like my sister getting a brand-new car when I got a used Oldsmobile Custom Cruiser station wagon, or the fact that my parents paid for her wedding while I paid for mine. But I also like to think that in twenty years, when my mom is at some totally depressing hospital unable to understand the breathing exercise where she has to blow a ball to the top of a plastic, I'll be three thousand miles away in Los Angeles, while my sister is stuck visiting every day, wishing she'd never asked for that cotton candy machine.

David and Jono Kohan
4.16.77
Los Angeles, California

"I told the Bar Mitzvah planner that I liked the Police and Van Halen and so this cake was born. After my Bar Mitzvah, what was left was stuffed into our freezer only to be unearthed three years later at my sixteenth birthday and devoured by my slightly inebriated friends."

Jeremy Kroll
4.28.84
Rye, New York

Nigel Bennett
4.11.81
Liverpool, England

Ari Osur
6.13.87
Fairfield Sheraton
Fairfield, New Jersey

"Rick from Music King performed at every party in Columbus. My mom wanted to veer away from the norm and shipped in a DJ from Toledo. The gamble backfired—the purple spandex bulge scared the kids so my mom had to take the set list into her own hands."

Jules Shell
4.21.90
Winding Hollow Country Club
Columbus, Ohio

LAST NIGHT A DJ SAVED MY LIFE

Listen up to your local DJ—you better hear what he's got to say
—Indeep

The first superstar DJ's of the modern era were neither Carl Cox nor Paul Oakenfold. Before these two gents were toilet trained, pioneers like Johnny James and Richie Hart were redefining the way we celebrated, putting Bar Mitzvah bands out of business up and down the east coast in the process. Like the baseball stars in the old Negro leagues, they never got the respect they deserved during their careers, but this fact does nothing to undermine their contribution to modern democracies across the globe. A direct line can be traced between them and the techno explosion of the late nineties. Long before Ecstasy and Red Bull, they learned to spin the crowd right round like a record, baby, armed only with a meager supply of Glo-sticks, crazee hats, and punk rock tinsel wigs.

To the untrained eye, this may appear to be a lineup of cheeseball hustlers, but don't let the purple spandex fool you. Above all these gentlemen were master psychologists who could render anybody they chose powerless to resist their command with a deft flick of a fader changing the tempo from "The Safety Dance" to "Total Eclipse of the Heart." These men lived the life, and had it all: the clothes, the women, and the money. Their after-parties were the stuff of legend. Once their equipment was safely packed up in the back of the truck, they would round up the party motivators and a lucky sprinkling of guests, whisk them back to their bachelor pads, and continue the party Caligula-style. True professionals that they were, they would wake up early the next morning without fail and set up for a Sunday lunchtime Bat Mitzvah and do it all over again.

Johnny James, DJ
Circa 1989
New Jersey

HOW TO ROCK OUT

By SAM SPIEGEL (A.K.A. DJ SQUEAK E. CLEAN)

The DJ has been around for as long as history can recall. He has been an integral figure in the formation of civic society as a whole, and played an even bigger part of what we have come to know as the Jewish religion. To fully understand Jewish history, we must come to understand the paramount role that the DJ plays in it, the Bar Mitzvah DJ in particular, and how he has supplanted the rabbi as the centrifugal force of the religion.

Consider the question: What is a Bar Mitzvah without a DJ? A bunch of zit-faced Jewish teenagers, awkwardly standing around thinking about all of the dirty things that they want to do to each other, but feeling too scared of rejection to act on any of their illicit desires. A DJ brings the music, and just like at many other social gatherings with sexually charged participants, music becomes the catalyst of social/sexual interaction. All the brats can get their grind on each other, or even their awkward joke dance, thus loosening the tension created by their desire. This will ultimately lead to more relaxed relations, kissing, making out, alcohol abuse; underage, unprotected sex, teen pregnancy, sexually transmitted diseases, substance abuse, eventual drug addiction, homelessness, and HIV, in others words, all of the things that a thirteen-year-old with any sense is interested in.

Now that the function of the DJ has been made obvious to my dear readers, I should like to expound upon the real purpose of our little section on the Bar Mitzvah DJ, which is informative, or more so, tutorial. There are certain songs, which as a member of the very top echelon of Bar Mitzvah DJ's, I have come to discover work their magic upon the Bar Mitzvah crowd to the greatest effect. In the DJ industry, we might call these songs "crowd-pleasers." As a master of the DJ craft and a devout student of human nature, my interest was peaked by this phenomenon. Why is it that these few songs could wreak so much havoc upon an unsuspecting crowd of oversexed pubescents and uptight parents? I took it upon myself to delve into the minds of my subjects, to scrutinize and analyze their every thought and movement, and you, as the reader, have the divine pleasure of reading my results (for the first time published herein).

Y.M.C.A.—The Village People

The first and most obvious song that I studied was brought to us by gay America. I state this fact not because I harbor ill will or prejudice against our nation's homosexual culture, but to demonstrate the subconscious affect that this song has on a crowd. Women love the flamboyant gay culture because it's glamorous and fabulous, and it's all about panache and posture. This is what excites the adolescent girls when they hear this song. The boys' hearts flutter when they hear the song's opening horns for another reason, however. All of the built-up repression that festers in the mind of a teenage boy can be alleviated with three minutes of flamboyantly joyous music. "Y.M.C.A." gives the teenage boy (or his dad) the ability to indulge in his man-love fantasies in a socially acceptable way. This, coupled with the fact that awkward teenagers like to be told exactly how to dance so they won't stray off the cool or goofy path, makes "Y.M.C.A." a guaranteed hit. Which leads me to the next song.

The Electric Slide

A surefire winner. Not only is it a song that these miserable brats hear at every birthday party and school dance, but everyone knows the dance too, and unless a kid is crippled, he's going to be able to dance along, fit in (one of the primary objectives of a thirteen-year-old), and look like he knows how to dance. This song can bridge the popularity, ethnicity, and even the clique barriers that normally separate peers at that age, and can get everyone dancing and sweating to the same beat. This song is all-conquering and all-powerful.

Salt 'N' Pepa—Push It

"Push It" is the ultimate social lubricant. The tenure of this song in our pop culture (since the early eighties) makes it just acceptable from the parents' point of view to play at a Bar Mitzvah. This doesn't take away from the fact that the song is about casual sexual encounters on the dance floor, and the panting in the beat along with the lyrics are enough to cause excitement in the skivvies of any pubescent. I usually like to play this song later in the night when the parents have retired to their tables, and the kids' curiosity can be explored.

Madonna—Vogue

Madonna, in her time, was the apex of sexuality in our culture. She was the subject of wet dreams for millions of teenage boys, and the envy of millions of girls. I know it. She graced me with my first nocturnal emission. Thank you, Madonna. That white outfit you were wearing was just so hot. Sorry . . . getting offtrack. Play the hottie. What's more is that all the ladies can imitate her gay backup dancers' vogue styles and live out their male-envy fantasies. Liberation!

Prince—Kiss

What's the story here? How could an androgynous being ooze so much sex appeal? This man is made to rock your Bar Mitzvah. Parents can relive their drugged-out party memories, and all the kids love the VH1 "Where Are They Now?" with Prince. He'll rip the dance floor to shreds, leaving all of the kiddies begging for more. Why? The answer lies in Lake Minnetonka.

Any Michael Jackson Song

Michael Jackson is the King of Pop. You are safe in assuming that in any party environment, Michael Jackson will blow the party up, especially with any song from *Off the Wall* or *Thriller.* The Bar Mitzvah is a perfect environment for Michael. I'm not even going to explore the correlation between his rocking the brats' bodies on the dance floor and his recent allegations of child molestation, but I think the relationship is obvious. He knows how to rock booty, and he's not going to stop until every adolescent is sweating to the beat.

Perhaps you will use this valuable information to rock your family members' Bar Mitzvah, or perhaps you will become your own Bar Mitzvah DJ and ascend to a life of glamour, debauchery, and making more money than God, like myself. But however you use it, know that you, as the DJ, are the apex of the Bar Mitzvah, the focal point, and without you, there is no way for the child to become an adult. The Bar Mitzvah DJ has a social responsibility to the Jewish community, and one has to be mindful of this great duty that has been placed on him. Use your power to the greatest of good. Aaiight?

So, now that you've got your basics . . . go *rock* those kids. . . .

DJ Squeak E. Clean's Tried and Tested Crowd-Pleasers

"Ice Ice Baby'
"Push It"
Michael Jackson Medley
"Wild Thing"
"Bust a Move"
"Good Vibrations"
"Kiss"
"Pour Some Sugar on Me"
"Paradise City"
"Love Shack"
"The Electric Slide"
"Let's Get It On"
"Bad Boys"
"Like a Virgin" mixed into "Vogue"
"Staying Alive"

Eric Rubenstein
2.25.84
Tamarac, Florida

WE DON'T HAVE TO TAKE OUR CLOTHES OFF

So come on baby, won't you show some class
Why you want to move so fast
—Jermaine Stewart

There's an urban legend that says Chuck Barris originally conceived of *The Gong Show* while attending a Bar Mitzvah on Long Island in the early seventies. This photo series suggests there may be truth to this tale. While the Jewish people can lay no claim to having invented karaoke, it appears they did enough amateur entertaining in the seventies and eighties to prove that the very celebrated Neils—Sedaka and Diamond—as well as Barbra, were not one-off aberrations.

But what were their parents thinking? They were fully aware of the scale of the emotional trauma their beloved offspring had experienced during their trial by fire at the local synagogue in the morning. Yet they were still willing to compound the damage by thrusting them up on stage with an accordion, a Fender, or just their glass-piercing voice for company.

From the look of the photos, some of the characters were clearly terrified by the ordeal. Others seem like they strode up and seized the moment as if grabbing that microphone would change the course of their lives (and by the look of things, it might have done, but not always for the better). It should be noted that some of those featured here did indeed go on to achieve great things in the entertainment industry and to contribute to what we know as modern popular culture. Others can currently be found selling double scoops at Dairy Queen.

MADONNA AND CHILD

By SHAUN SPERLING

My mom and I were shopping one day and I saw these Madonna earrings, in the shape of a record. I said, "If my theme was Madonna, we could give those to all my girlfriends." My mom said, "Well, I guess if that's what you are really in to, the theme should be Madonna."

My father loved the theme. Do you believe that it never crossed my family's mind that I was gay through this whole process? I think my dad always just thought I wanted her. But in any case, he helped with the entire process and loved everything, from the dance to my speech that ended with "Now strike a pose and let's get to it!"

Being the kid that I was, I didn't want to enter the reception like all my friends who were called to the Torah before me. I was so obsessed with the song "Vogue," when I got the tape, my sister and I would stand at the stereo and listen to it again and again to learn every word. Then, when the video came out, I watched it over and over until I learned every move. Naturally, we came up with the idea for me to enter the room after "becoming a man" and do a dance to "Vogue." Every day after school, my sister would coach me to do the dance to perfection. She would scream things at me like "Stronger arms!" or "Pose strong!"

My mom came up with the idea to have Madonna painted on the back of my shirt so that when I was dancing, I could dramatically throw my jacket off and reveal the "artwork." It was so comforting knowing that while I was reading from the Torah for the first time a big gaudy picture of Madonna was right there on my back. As a coda, let me tell you this: my DJ, Lou Loiben, ended up dating my sister Kelli. Twelve years later, they are married and have a baby, Mackenzi.

Nicky Siegel
10.12.85
Tammy Brook Country Club
Alpine, New Jersey

Julie Hermelin
9.5.80
Southfield, Michigan

JJ Smith
4.13.91
Ridgeway Country Club
White Plains, New York

"I always chose to play the piano with dear relatives mere inches from my body."

Scott Jacoby
10.31.84
Westchester, New York

HERE BY POPULAR DEMAND
Late Night
WITH
BRETT GELMAN
★★★★★
"Certain to be one of the best sons of all time"
— Mom & Dad
"Totally awesome"
— Meredith
"Lots of laughs and a true delight"
— Grandma Kaye
"Really has his act together"
— Grandma Reva, Grandpa Ben
ONE NIGHT ONLY
We Invite You
To Share In Our Happiness
When Our Son
Brett Clifford
Is Called To The Torah
As A Bar Mitzvah
Saturday, October 28, 1989
At 4:30 In The Afternoon
Congregation B'NAI TORAH
2789 Oak Street
Highland Park, Illinois
Celebrate With Us
Following The Service
At
Allgauer's Hotel
2855 N. Milwaukee Avenue
Northbrook, Illinois
Candace and Ira Gelman
Brett has the honor of spiritually sharing his Bar Mitzvah with Nikolay Goldenberg of the Soviet Union and Desie Atakilt of Ethiopia

LATE NIGHT WITH BRETT GELMAN

By BRETT GELMAN

Junior high sucked really bad for me. If someone laughed at what I was wearing or tripped me in the hall, I considered that a good day. At least they were taking time out of their popular schedules to pay attention to me.

My parents had a sense of this situation and they knew they had one chance to turn it around. Their mission was to make my Bar Mitzvah count. And they did.

My mother was the commandant of the whole operation. She had the idea of naming my day of days "Late Night With Brett Gelman." And she swore we would do things for this holy event that no one had seen the likes of before, or would ever see again.

First off, she somehow found this guy in Las Vegas who had access to the head shot of every comedian under the sun, and more importantly, a giant book of celebrity addresses. My mom put both to good use as she wrote a letter to each comedian, informing them they were my favorite entertainer, and as it was my Bar Mitzvah, asking them if they would please sign the head shot she supplied and put it in the self-addressed envelope also included.

A couple of weeks later they starting coming in. At first a trickle, then a flood of eight-by-ten letters in the mail. George Burns, Bob Hope, Mel Brooks, Woody Allen, Richard Pryor, Gene Wilder, John Candy, Steve Martin, Lily Tomlin, Bill Cosby, and Don Rickles. Almost every comedian she had sent the letter and picture to had signed it (or their assistant had) and sent it back. Most of them wrote the standard "Happy Bar Mitzvah." But some got a little creative. None other than Mr. Arsenio Hall instructed me on his head shot to "Think Like A Winner." Oh, and I did, Mr. Hall. I did. These pictures would be the Bar Mitzvah tables'centerpieces. It made checking the mail one of the most exciting endeavors I have ever ventured on in my whole life.

By now, my mother was on a roll. Why make do with a flimsy invitation when a poster could be made? A giant poster with a picture of me in a top hat and tails, standing under a huge headline: "Late Night With Brett Gelman." She hired a professional photographer to take the black-and-white photo, and next to me were my reviews. Reviews like "He's a real star"—Grandma Reva and Grandpa Ben. And above the reviews was my rating, not four, but five stars. And I'll be damned if my mother wasn't struck with another brilliant idea. Why mail these special invitations, when you could deliver them door to door? She made every detail down to the delivery of the invitations both tasteful and personal.

Come the big day, and all reports suggested that the service was beautiful, but the party at a local hotel was where the action happened. For the cocktail hour all the kids did karaoke, while the adults got quietly hammered. I faked people out by singing karaoke in the blue pin-striped suit I had worn during the temple service. But, about halfway through the cocktail hour my dad discreetly sneaked me out of the room and took me to a secure location—a hotel suite he had rented. In this room my top hat and tails were lying on the bed, waiting for me to make my transformation from Brett Gelman, Mr. Nobody, to B.G., Mr. Showtime. And as I put on my royal party garbs, I felt that change take over me. I was extremely nervous, but the wonderfully classic feel of the tux and top hat, coupled with the pride in my father's eyes, washed that anxiety away. I knew I would kill 'em. Not with jokes, but with who I was. All these popular kids who had always snubbed me. Whom I so wanted to be, tonight would all want to be me. The Jewish Prince of Comedy.

My father and I then snuck back downstairs for my grand entrance, and while he proudly took his seat, I hid behind the doorway and waited to be announced. Again the anxiety returned. This was it! My big moment. This would make me or break me. I would leave tonight the star I knew I could be, or the outcast I always had been. I was sweating. (I don't know if it was necessarily from the anxiety, though. I used to eat a lot of cheese.) I could feel all my guests anticipating my arrival. Then that silence hit. That split second of silence before the storm. My anxiety level escalated tenfold, but as I ran my hand across the brim of my felt crown, I knew that anxiety would be transformed into pure, unbridled performance energy.

My moment came. The DJ played *The Tonight Show* theme (I know it was "Late Night with Brett Gelman" but *The Tonight Show*'s theme is catchier) and announced into the microphone, "Heeeeeeeeeeeeeeeerrrrrrrre's Brett!" And out I jumped. I didn't even feel my feet touch the floor as the applause roared. I grabbed the microphone as if it was my royal scepter, and as I spoke into it, I was able to ignore how feminine my voice sounded as it rang through the giant stereo speakers. Insecurity was conquered by the surprise I felt in the room. Besides my parents, I don't think anyone thought that I was capable of what I had just done. Especially myself. I had taken stage, and received the affirmation I had hungered for my whole life. The rest of the night was pure gravy. It was all down hill from here.

"I'm giving the standard Bar Mitzvah speech here but was thinking about the electric guitar I was going to buy with my parents' friends' money. I'm dressed in what I thought a cowboy would wear. I convinced myself it was cool with its Guns N' Roses/Skid Row vibe. There was a girl there named Pixie. I wrote songs about her. She was my first muse."

Ben Lee
8.24.91
Sydney, Australia,

David Measer
5.5.84
Chasen's Restaurant
Hollywood, California

ROCK STAR AXE-GOD

By DAVID MEASER

"You need a theme. Everyone has one. It's kind of like your image." The voice was my mother's, tinged with competitive vigor and a caffeinated edge. I was twelve and a half years old. My image, as far as I could tell, revolved mostly around Atari Missile Command, hating my sister, and *Dukes of Hazzard* reruns. Coming up with a theme was a difficult task. I liked ice cream, what did that say about me? I had recently started taking classical guitar lessons. Maybe my theme could have something to do with music?

"That's it!" my parents exclaimed, and began writing the checks.

And I began making decisions. My mother and I went on excursions to scout locations for the reception. My father and I snuck into a few Bar Mitzvah receptions to listen to prospective bands. I picked the Sound Company because of their expertise with the Duran Duran catalog. My grandfather chipped in after he found a crate of junked 45s in a dumpster in Hollywood (Men at Work's "Overkill" must have been selling surprisingly badly) and we began to craft elaborate centerpieces from the little records. It was the most exciting time of my life. Even my sister helped out by suggesting that, rather than table numbers, we name each table after a band. On our list: the Thompson Twins, Culture Club, David Bowie, the Clash, Oingo Boingo, Duran Duran, Wham, and the Go-Go's. Then our erstwhile party planner suggested that I incorporate the current vogue of celebrity impersonators into my musical theme. No sooner said than done.

A Michael Jackson look-alike was promptly hired to moonwalk and lip-sync the words to "Billy Jean." I very nearly wept.

After I'd decided on the theme, I began to realize that something was different. I was involved. Up until then, nearly all of the decisions in my life were left to the grown-ups: the schools I attended, the clothes I wore, what I ate for breakfast. But now, big decisions suddenly required my input. My interests actually mattered. Do you prefer spinach blintzes or chicken skewers as hors d'oeuvres? Would inviting the principal of your school increase your chances of getting into a good college? Is cousin Eleanor far enough removed from her 12-step program to be around an open bar? My opinions would have ramifications on adults. It seemed that the entire community of family, friends, and party profiteers were looking at me in a whole different way. They seemed to be treating me . . . well, like a man. And they were collectively telling me: "We think you're cool."

And I was intent on staying cool. It was that message that led me to devise my own thematic climax to my themed event. Alive with the idea that my Bar Mitzvah was an image-defining event, I opted to do something very much out of character. I plotted to rise above the shyness and awkwardness that had marked my entire youth and do something new. On the night I would become a man, I would shed my classical guitar and pick up an electric guitar and jam with the band.

My decision to rock out at my Bar Mitzvah was motivated in part by the traditional lure of musicians everywhere: girls. Over the course of my thirteenth year, I began to notice them. And I became acquainted with a new feeling in my stomach—kind of a combination of hunger and fear—when they were around. Girls were now about a foot taller than me, spoke in mellifluous tones, smelled really nice, and had boobs. I wanted to slow dance to the Thompson Twins' "Hold Me Now" with as many of them as possible. And I just knew that a few power chords from that Fender Telecaster would make it all possible.

The moment came shortly after the hora but before "Rock Lobster." Guests had just finished their chicken à l'orange and had already taken their picture with the slightly lethargic Michael Jackson impersonator. The break dancing half hour hadn't produced any notable injuries, and most of my friends were back in the banquet room after all attempts to find cigarettes had failed. My father made his speech, with allusions to the price of the reception and a joke about the health of the bond market, which he had been carefully crafting since my birth.

When the leader of the Sound Company called me to the stage, nobody seemed quite sure what was happening. It was clearly not Eighties Bar Mitzvah protocol. Perhaps he was making a speech, an announcement, a teary thank-you to his parents? Then the bandleader handed me that big, gleaming electric guitar. There was something like a collective gasp. I strapped the thing over my shoulder and looked around.

My Bar Mitzvah audience came alive with emotion. And they were all looking at me. Drunk fortysomething friends of my father's and their drunk twentysomething girlfriends cheered wildly. Eastern European relatives, their pockets loaded with dinner rolls and Sweet 'n Low packets, howled approvingly. My family looked on with nervous pride. My friends whistled. The girls giggled. They adjusted their hair. I was the center of their attention. This was cool.

I paused for a moment, then hit the first chords of "Pinball Wizard." As my pick hit the strings for the first time, and the sounds began to echo from my guitar, I knew my life had just changed a little bit. I was somehow reborn. For that one night, I was a rock star.

"We thought we were so cool, all eyes on our California Raisin costumes. The excitement wore off when I realized that my seventh grade crush was now seeing me in a large sack. I quickly took it off and dumped it on the dance floor. Minutes later, out of the corner of my eye, I see my dad, in all his glory, proudly dancing in the very costume I had just disposed of."

Barri Budin
4.21.90
South Orange, New Jersey

"I spent the entire evening with one hand on my strapless dress to keep from flashing my family and friends."

Lisa Rosenblum
4.29.89
Radisson Suites
Palm Beach Gardens, Florida

THREE FEET HIGH AND RISING

How high's the water, Mama?
It's three feet high and rising.
—De La Soul

Few grown men understood the mind of the child as well as Walt Disney. But even he underestimated the tradition of the chair lift. When Disneyland was in the early stages of construction, Uncle Walt designed an attraction called the Hebrew Hair Raiser. Admittedly basic in construction, the ride consisted of five college students dressed up in Goofy outfits plopping the customers on a chair and thrusting them skywards. Much to his surprise the Raiser did not focus-group well. For most of the children it was a terrifying experience during which one in seven upchucked their corndogs. We recount this story to prove that the power of the chair-lifting experience should not be underestimated.

The chair lift tradition was originally the sole domain of the Jewish wedding. But in the late sixties it began to be inculcated as a core part of the Bar/Bat Mitzvah ritual as more and more mothers began to fear they may not live to see the day their daughters would walk down the aisle. For the child, the experience was often an intoxicating mix of omnipotence and self-confidence. In the midst of puberty, with their bodies whacked out of synch and their minds filled with desires they don't quite understand, they are surrounded by their family and community who in one act, symbolically shout out, "You are cool. Go for it." When it comes to the parents' turn, the ordeal is a little less of a thrill. Dad, the accountant, tries to unconvincingly pull off the look of a cruiserweight who has just won a big fight. Mom can't help but reenact the face she pulled during the act of conception.

Aaron Judah Bondaroff
3.17.90
New York, New York

"I am getting the most action I had ever received in this shot. Hence the extreme widening of the mouth. I had never had three grown men look up my skirt before. Two of them were my closest friends' fathers. That makes it even dirtier."

Elissa Bowes
10.13.90
The Waterfall Room, The Sheraton
Wayne, New Jersey

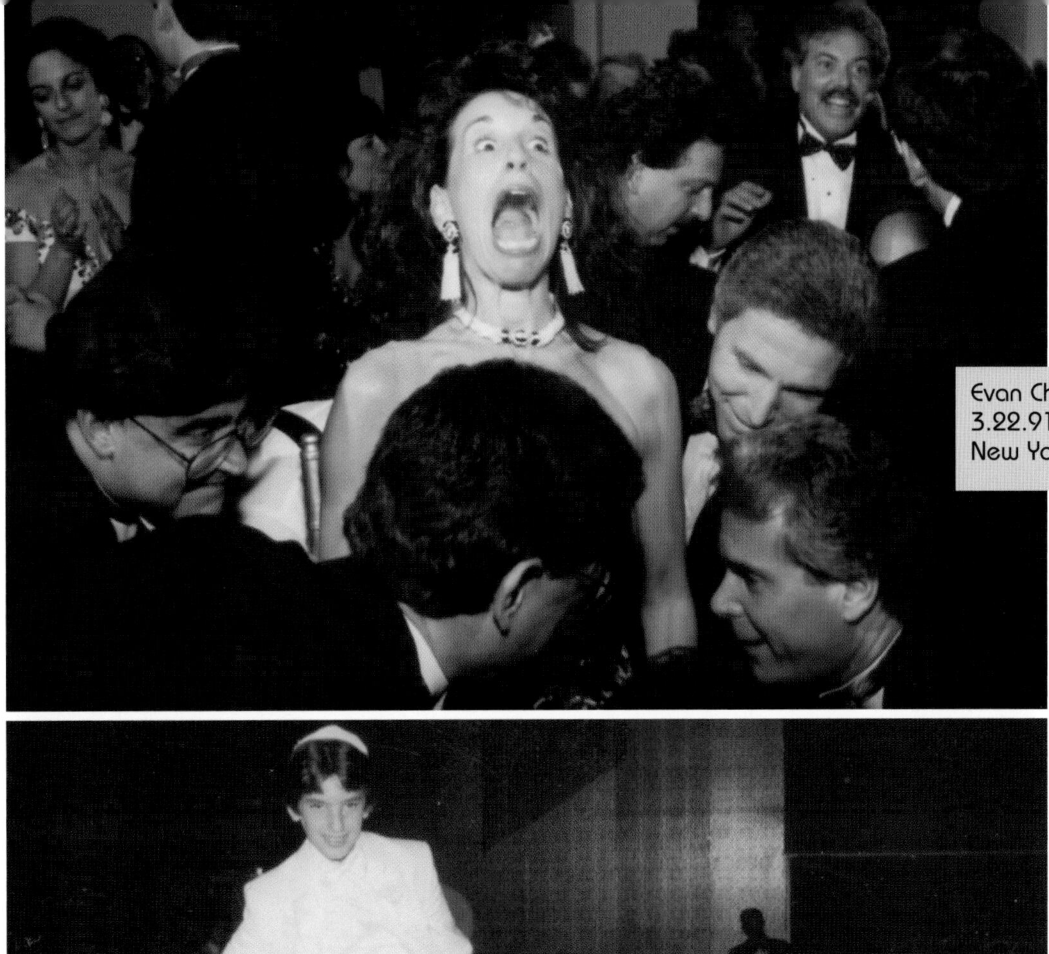

Evan Chadakoff
3.22.91
New York, New York

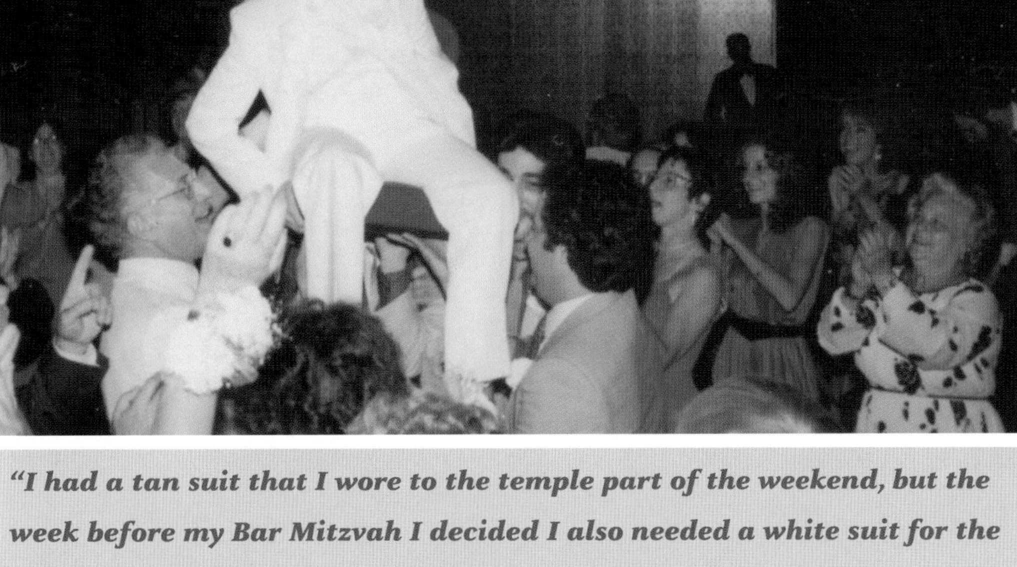

"I had a tan suit that I wore to the temple part of the weekend, but the week before my Bar Mitzvah I decided I also needed a white suit for the party. I was a big Steve Martin fan and he always wore the white suit, not to mention Travolta in* Saturday Night Fever.*"

Robert Cohen
6.27.82
Brooklyn, New York

Gary Benerofe
5.12.90
Bridgewaters
South Street Seaport
New York, New York

THE SHOW

Ladies and Gentleman . . . the most exciting stage show you've ever witnessed . . .
—Doug E. Fresh

By the level of giddy glee they are emoting, you would never guess they were paid to be there. But yes, everyone from Michael Jackson and Madonna impersonators, to people on stilts and women dressed up as medium format cameras have succumbed to the opening of Dad's wallet and appeared as star turns at Bar/Bat Mitzvahs—another reason they may be perfect to examine the highs and lows and evolution of popular culture.

Let us take a minute to pay some respect to the hired dancers, or "party motivators" as they prefer to be called. They may look like women of ill-repute, but please believe us when we tell you that most were highly trained operatives, competitively recruited from Ivy League schools or straight off the set of *Club MTV.* Each came with niche social specialties like arousing Grandpa, ensuring Grandma felt listened to, or making the Bar Mitzvah boy imagine he had left his own party and arrived at one of Charlie Sheen's by some uncanny mistake. Their job must rank as one of the toughest in show business—coaxing even the most flatulent and corporeal to put down the nosebag, momentarily forget about the arson they were planning to save the family business, and, for one song at a time, persuading them they were Leroy from *Fame,* or Deney Terrio from *Dance Fever.*

"I don't know where we got the band from in Bexley. I don't know if they ever played another Bar Mitzvah."

Mike Epstein
5.29.89
Columbus, Ohio

"This is Ozzie Newsome (right), pro-football Hall of Fame tight end from the Cleveland Browns, and Brian Brennan, the former wide receiver for the Browns. I was thinking 'NFL, here I come! I can't wait till my bust is next to Ozzie's in the Hall of Fame.'"

Seth Singerman
4.21.90
Beechmont Country Club
Pepperpike, Ohio

PETE BEST'S BAR MITZVAH

By MARK RONSON

My stepdad, Mick, was born Church of England. But he wanted in pretty bad and was more than happy to have a traditional Jewish wedding when he married my mother, Anne. He was a good sport at the holidays too, reciting back the Hebrew as we dictated it in front of the candles. My sisters and I would amuse ourselves to no end by making him unwittingly say things like "Baruch ata adonai mecca-lecca-hi mecca-heini-ho, barai pari goonie goo goo" (we were equal fans of both *Pee-Wee's Playhouse* and Eddie Murphy's "Delirious").

The coolest thing was that Mick was also a rock star. He founded the group Foreigner in the late seventies and wrote AM radio anthems like "Hot Blooded" and "Cold As Ice." In the eighties, he churned out a bunch more hits—including "I Want to Know What Love Is," which he wrote for my mother and is now heard in post offices and supermarkets hourly. Well, my Bar Mitzvah window just happened to coincide with his '88 Agent Provocateur world tour, so after moving the dates around and switching synagogues a few times, we finally nailed down a date and a place with an after-party set for Tavern on the Green.

The day itself was like a rock concert. The venue was Park Avenue Synagogue. Doors were open at 11 A.M. I had a local act as an opener—the impressively precise if uninspired circumcision of a hapless infant. Then the emcee, Rabbi Einseidler, brought me to the stage, introduced me, and I rocked my haftarah with ease.

However, I was a Prince fan, and just like him, I knew that I would save my best performance for the more intimate crowd at the after-show party. So around 10 P.M., after some speeches whose only purpose I was sure was to embarrass me in front of hot eighth-grade girls, Mick and I took to the bandstand. He picked up his guitar, I got behind the drum kit, and we launched into "Hot Blooded," bringing the heavy-metal fire to Tavern on the Green like never before. It is worth noting, this was more than a decade before the White Stripes had even thought to electrify a crowd with just drums and guitar. Jews and non-Jews both prayed to the gods of rock that night, the only problem was that we never rehearsed an encore.

"We had a game show for the kids, and the winner was allowed time in the money machine. The whole thing was rigged, of course, so I came out the winner."

Abbey Orlofsky
11.9.91
Brae Burn Country Club
Purchase, New York

"In this business, there are wanna-bes, mighta-beens, coulda-beens, shoulda-beens, woulda-beens, and a whole lot of has-beens."

Uncle Marty
Enchanted Parties
Circa 1988

"Celebrity look-alikes seem to go hand in hand for Bar and Bat Mitzvahs. I am lucky Madonna has stayed hip for kids that age so they do not mess with me like they do with other look-alikes. I've seen a George Michael near tears once because he was taking so much verbal abuse from the kids."

Bella Vlasis
Madonna impersonator
Circa 1990
Los Angeles, California

"Sven and Marushka, the greatest fire-eaters/limbo-dancers in the Tri-State area. Sven made a pass at my mother that night, and Marushka allegedly got to second base with one of my thirteen-year-old friends."

Andrew Goldberg
3.7.91
Mamaroneck Beach & Yacht Club
Mamaroneck, New York

Gary Benerofe
5.12.90
Bridgewaters
South Street Seaport
New York, New York

Michael Kinsit
2.22.85
Miami, Florida

Craig Benerofe
11.22.86
The Manhattan Club
New York, New York

David Measer
5.5.84
Chasen's Restaurant
Hollywood, California

Rachel Slaw
5.21.91
Crown Plaza
White Plains, New York

Y.M.C.A.

They have everything for young men to enjoy,
You can hang out with all the boys.
—The Village People

There is little that better promotes multigenerational bonding nor ensnares reluctant diners on the dance floor than the group dance. Jews know any of the following songs better than they know the words to the Israeli national anthem: "Y.M.C.A.," "The Electric Slide," "London Bridge," and "The Chicken Dance." And after the crowd was allowed an appropriate amount of time to digest the plate of food they had just devastated, they were given the opportunity to loosen their limbs via a couple rounds of limbo, lip-synching, or that competition unique to the Bar/Bat Mitzvah circuit, Coke and Pepsi, which is to Jews what the sport of curling is to the Canadians.

But beneath the surface frivolity evident in these photos, the emotional engines were still churning for many. One of our contributors, Jordanna Fraiberg, captured this beautifully as she relived the emotional trauma of this phase of the merrymaking: "I had a pit in my stomach as the night progressed and my skills of social navigation were put to the test. There wasn't just the fear of not being asked to dance to a slow song, but the humiliation of not keeping up with the latest moves in the group dance, or not knowing the words to a current hit. It's a myth that everyone is included in a group dance. While exclusion is not as overt, there are subtle ways one can feel left out, and in some ways, that feeling is worse than being alone because you feel invisible too."

Josh Weinberg
9.9.79
Woodbury Country Club
Long Island, New York

Risa Jaslow
1983
B'nai Israel
Staten Island, New York

Anonymous
circa 1989
New York, New York

CONFESSIONS OF A WASPY JEW

By PETER HYMAN

Thanks to several complementary factors—my parents' relaxed feelings toward mixed marriage, a shared fascination with living life as though it were a chapter in *The Great Gatsby,* and their insistence that their offspring attend private secondary schools until the recitation of both Latin and the rules of lacrosse became second nature—I hold the slightly confusing position of being a WASPy Jew.

By this I mean that I am, at the same time, compelled by habit to dress like Alex P. Keaton's understudy in beat-up khakis, aging Izods, and a near religious affinity to Sperry topsiders, and neurotically concerned about monitoring the most minute details of my physical well-being with a thorough checkup every six months, to the consternation of my internist (and whomever does his insurance paperwork).

In short, my WASPy tendencies illustrate themselves in external ways, while my internal landscape is all Jew. And while this trait does provide me with the confidence to walk around knowing that I am properly attired should I be kidnapped and held hostage at a cocktail party in Newport, Rhode Island, my overly analytical predisposition brings a fair amount of frustration to those who spend time with me in any atmosphere that requires the making of decisions.

This duality showed itself in sharpest relief during the Bar Mitzvah years. While I understood the mechanics of the sacred ceremony from my spotty Sunday school education, I was not fully of that world, showing up at receptions in a seersucker suit and penny loafers, worn without socks. And despite the somewhat softening influence *The Official Preppy Handbook* was having at that time, dressing like a young Tom Wolfe did not play well with the under-fifteen set in suburban Detroit during the early Reagan years. My cause was not aided by the fact that I was predisposed toward shyness and conversations about books involving maritime adventures. The seventh-grade cuties I was trying to make it to second base with were not all that receptive to opening lines that referred to Melville, even if the young man saying it happened to be wearing a boater.

Yet despite these obvious handicaps I was able to cobble together a respectable run between 1980 and 1983 (like Pete Rose, I was less a pure hitter than I was a guy who managed to get up to bat often), owing to an uncanny ability to do the hustle like nobody's business. Thanks to years of forced ballet and tap classes (undertaken, of course, to improve my balance for more manly, cleat-based endeavors) and a complete lack of awareness of how foolish I looked, I was something of a puberty-era Deney Terrio (sans the chest hair and *Dance Fever* dancers). And while this talent has waned in recent years, it did serve me well at the time, especially in the gentle blue eyes of Marla Levitsky.

Marla was a playground fantasy come to life, with her foxy features, feathered hair and Fiorucci jeans. While we had passed each other in the hallways at school, our first meaningful encounter took place at Danny Rubin's Bar Mitzvah, a gala, *Star Wars*-themed affair held high atop one of Detroit's most infamous landmarks, the Renaissance Center (which, true to the early eighties, featured the requisite rotating restaurant). Danny, more a sci-fi fan than a music lover, had opted for a DJ instead of a band, which played to my hustle-based strengths. Having made eye contact with Marla during the Torah reading and once again at the sweets table, I knew it was merely a matter of time before I encountered her on the faux-parquet floor.

The only question in my mind was this: Slow dance or fast-paced disco number? I had secretly requested both types of songs (the DJ knew my older brothers, so I was able to rely on the vicarious sense of cool that came with the association), assuring myself a good half step on my competition—Eric Solomon, with his flashy gold chain and chai pendant, and Jason Roth, the best Jewish athlete in school (this, of course, is not saying much, but you get the idea). I was more a ballad man myself, partial to "Stairway to Heaven," the holy grail of slow dances, with thirteen-plus minutes of adolescent fumbling. My strategy was to wait until I heard the first few A-minor licks from Jimmy Page's Les Paul #1 guitar, and then sweep Marla into a warm, Led Zeppelin-driven embrace.

As it happened, the DJ sold me out. Before I had a chance to make a move, the backstabbing longhair came over the loudspeaker to announce that it was time for the "snowball." Under the strict terms of the snowball dance (popular in the Midwest), the rules that have guided coed interaction since the biblical ages are turned upside down: The girls ask the boys to dance. This role reversal gives rise to a host of issues, functioning as an instant popularity contest and leaving one exposed to the stinging humiliation of being the last boy standing.

It was thus somewhat shocking when Marla, dazzling in her purple taffeta Norma Kamali party gown, grabbed my hand to pull me onto the dance floor without so much as a salutation or query as to my current level of availability. Beginning a habit that would mark my interaction with Jewish women for years to come, I followed dutifully in her wake. As it turned out, she liked the funny, preppy way I dressed, and the fact that I did not act like the rest of the boys. She did, however, request that I wear socks with my loafers on any and all future dates. I am not sure where Marla Levitsky is today, but for that moment (and, if I can brag, most of the next semester) we found pure bliss.

Dara Osur
3.17.90
Wayne, New Jersey

Shari Cantor
11.8.86
Columbus, Ohio

THE BAR MITZVAH AND GEO-POLITICS

By GIDEON YAGO

My Bar Mitzvah was pre-grunge. February 22, 1991, which was the same day that we technically won the first Gulf War. It was when the Iraqi army surrendered. Because there is a huge portion of my family and *mishpacha* who is Israeli that had come over rather than to wait for a scud missile attack, it was a particularly tense period for my family. Everybody was watching the news and radically aware of the threats to Israel. My Torah portion was called Zahor. It was about remembering what the Amalakites did to you and kicking ass, which was particularly bloody and violent. It was all about God having Saul go out there and kick the shit out of the Amalakites, so there was this whole war theme going on throughout the entire affair. They threw candy at the bimah and my rabbi made some joke about that being an air assault or something.

We did my Bar Mitzvah party at a Christian community center after the service. We did not want to rent out a big dining hall and have everyone in a taffeta dress surrounded by Star of David ice carvings or anything like that. We settled for renting a Ms. Pac-Man machine, a basketball hoop, and a dance floor with the cheesy Bar Mitzvah DJ playing Boyz II Men and C&C Music Factory and all the Queens Classics. But it got disrupted at nine o'clock, when my uncle Sheldon came running in saying, "The war is over, they surrendered, they surrendered." I remember them making an announcement like, "Can we kill the music. Just want to let you guys know we won the war, they are officially conceding. There is no longer a threat of scuds." That was a big deal for all of the Israelis who were there. Then there was a limbo contest after that and the music went right back on.

Michael Larsen
5.27.73
Regency House
Jamaica, Queens, New York

OLYMPIAN

By MATT GOLDICH

Every Bar Mitzvah features two main athletic competitions—the limbo and Coke and Pepsi. Of the two, I was always better at the limbo. This was mostly due to my late growth spurt. As a thirteen-year old, I was much smaller than most of my peers, and for the first few rounds of a limbo contest, I could sneak under the pole with little or no effort. As the limbo stick got lower and lower, however, those of us who were simply short were separated from the truly minuscule—people like Shari Krevitz, who couldn't have been more than four feet tall and made the science of limbo look ridiculously easy. Because of Shari, I rarely won a limbo contest—but I did know how to lose with panache. Facial contortions, flailing limbs, and celebratory end zone–style dances were all a part of my repertoire. If I couldn't win the game, I made sure I was at least going to win the crowd over.

Coke and Pepsi was not my forte. For those of you who have never had the pleasure of putting on a suit and dress shoes and running back and forth across the scuffed floor of a synagogue ballroom, the game is pretty simple. Each participant pairs up with somebody. One is deemed Coke, the other Pepsi. When your soda is called, you run across the room and sit in your partner's lap. One person is eliminated in each round until only one pair is left awkwardly crouching in formal wear.

Certain DJ's would try and complicate the game by introducing new commands midway through like "7-Up" for switching places, or "Dr. Pepper" for tearing an ACL. I was just never that great at Coke and Pepsi. My response time was fine, but I just couldn't run in those damn formal shoes. Not that it mattered, anyway—the game was always rigged so that the Bar/Bat Mitzvah boy or girl and his or her partner won. That way, even the clumsiest Jewish youngster in the whole school would have at least one shining moment of quasi-athletic glory to cherish for decades to come.

Matt Wood
3.15.86
The Palladium
New York, New York

THE MESSAGE

A child is born with no state of mind
Blind to the ways of mankind
—Grand Master Flash

Break dancing may have been born on the streets, but it came of age in the cul de sacs and well-manicured lawns of suburban America. Hot off the sets of *Fresh Groove 2* and *Electric Boogaloo,* break-dancing troupes quickly established themselves as a hot commodity on the Bar and Bat Mitzvah circuit. Their appearance marked the time the party began to enter its final, more sordid phase, as the sight of the adorable kinder poppin', lockin', and doing the worm made everyone over the age of seventeen think about heading for the exit.

There is little in life more primitive, carnal, and uncoordinated than a bunch of Bar/Bat Mitzvah kids breakin' it down. These photographs appear like tribal mating rituals. Once the pros had showcased their style, it was time for the kids to ape their moves. Some had real skills, but many were just the boys who were too tall to limbo and unsyncopated for Coke and Pepsi, making their last desperate efforts to impress the female of the species. Their bodies flailing sweatily made the following statement "I am here. I am supple. I am white, but Goddamit, I have needs."

"A group of my guy friends who thought they had some breakin' skills commandeered the dance floor. The crowd ate it up. The two guys in front are Dean Gellar and Jon Palermo. They never made it as professional dancers."

Adam Smith
11.5.83
Ridgeway Country Club
White Plains, New York

THE "B" IN B-BOY REALLY MEANT BAR MITZVAH

By JOSH KUN

I didn't go through puberty until I was nearly seventeen, which had a few consequences. First, it meant that I could pull off wearing Ton Sur Ton sweatshirts and Guess jeans with the fold-down-and-button knee flaps far deeper into the eighties than they were ever meant to be worn. Second, it meant that my friends would sing "More Than a Woman" whenever I sat down at the lunch table. Third, it meant giving up the basketball team for books of Spanish poetry and a hook-rug pillow in the shape of a dachshund that I would feverishly work while I watched episodes of *CHiPs* and *Matt Houston* next to my mother. But most importantly, it meant that I could remain a great break-dancer. My thin wrists and nimble legs made popping, locking, and moonwalking effortless, and the fact that my waistline was tiny everywhere—everywhere—guaranteed a painless landing when I dropped to do the worm across somebody's hardwood floor.

If you were a ritzy private-school Jew on LA's Westside in the eighties, Bar Mitzvahs were break-dance Meccas. Sure you had to suffer through watching your uncles and aunts do choreographed line dances to Otis Day and the Knights' "Shout" and the B-52's' "Rock Lobster," and sure there was a limbo contest to get to and a round of Pepsi and 7-Up to compete in, but eventually the hour of the break dance would arrive. The band would hit those opening bass lines of "White Lines" (it was

the only hip-hop song Bar Mitzvah bands knew in the age before "U Can't Touch This") and the girls would rip off their panty hose (the surefire sign that any Bar or Bat Mitzvah was about to get serious) and the break-dance circle would instantly form (a natural formation for Jews used to dancing the hora in a moving circle) locking arms around shoulders and crossing one leg in front of the other as if we were about to leap into a head spin.

I break-danced at Bar Mitzvahs because it was trendy, not because I wanted to be a hip-hop kid. I'm sure Bar Mitzvahs saw their fair share of Mailerian white Negroes and haftarah homeboys, but for the most part, the Bar Mitzvah breakers in my Reform world weren't wiggers in training—no baggie pants, no fantasies of black orgasm, no yearnings for urban primitive ecstasy (in the days before hip-hop went mainstream, most of us were too Westside sheltered to even imagine black life or even have black friends we could fetishize). After all, the apex of my break-dancing days was my Bar Mitzvah year, 1984. Three years before Ice-T released *Rhyme Pays* and four years before NWA dropped *Straight Outta Compton,* 1984 was the year that *Breakin'* came out, the movie that established break dancing as a dance craze, not as a cultural ghetto pass. From 1984 on, if you were white and you break-danced, it didn't mean you were cool, it meant you were trendy. Break dancing was a way of separating ourselves from a mode of Jewishness that felt corny, overdetermined, and too removed from the lives we led during the week. It was a strategy of Jewish masking, being Jewish while pretending not to be, our way of participating in the expected rituals of our Jewishness while voicing—dancing—our distance from it.

I have seen only one document of my break-dance days. It's on the videotape of a friend's Bar Mitzvah. After the Michael Jackson impersonator tripped over his own feet during "Billie Jean," the floor cleared for a dance-off. The cameraman shoots it like it was *Dance Fever,* cutting between floor-spins and caterpillars and the faces of bemused parents. There was some strong talent out there, but let's just say that the sleeves on my button-down Polo oxford were rolled up high for a reason. The night was about to be mine.

Scott Jacoby
10.31.84
Westchester, New York

"In seventh grade, I had a crush on a guy who barely knew I existed, but was nice enough to slow dance with me a few times at my Bat Mitzvah party. Of course, by slow dancing I mean standing at an arm's length apart with our hands on each other's shoulders."—Eileen Quast

Shari Cantor
11.8.86
Columbus, Ohio

I THINK WE'RE ALONE NOW

We gotta hide what we're doin'
'Cause what would they say . . .
—Tiffany

What is this strange land I have come to, where girls tower over boys? The slow dance is what the Bar/Bat Mitzvah was really all about. What started in the morning with a reading from the Holy Scriptures, ended with a page or two ripped straight out of the early chapters of the *Karma Sutra.* The whole evening was a prelude to "Careless Whisper," a jockeying for position for "You Take My Breath Away." Oblivious to adult eyes the answers to the following questions had silently unfolded throughout the dinner serving and early dancing: Were you going to ask the guy or would he ask you? Who had your crush been moving on thus far and what had they been getting up to? How close would you be prepared to embrace come the moment of truth? What base did you tell your friends you were prepared to go for? What base were you really prepared to go for? How coolly were you prepared to react to the occasional ass grab?

No less an authority than *The Joy of Sex* admits that there are few more complex maneuvers to pull off successfully than the thirteen-year-old intimate moment at a Bar Mitzvah.

There were obstacles aplenty for both sexes. For the girls, this is where the hired dancers really mucked everything up. Any DJ knew that all it would take is the first few bars of "In the Air Tonight" to float over the dance floor to cause a prepubescent stampede of young boys understandably eager to have that special dance with one of the party motivators. From a budding playboy's perspective, the obstacles were all around. If the apple of your eye had a heart of gold, she could be otherwise engaged, taking pity on the class loser and giving him a "Sympathy Dance," three minutes of magic, the memory of which would allow him to extinguish the pain in his pants for years to come. The other threat was every girl's ultimate, the "Older Guy Dance" with a family friend who was fifteen or even sixteen, or with the DJ's assistant, Hans, who by virtue of being a student at the local community college could have his pick of the cherry bowl.

Peruse this gallery. See who had their moves down pat. See who was on the brink of getting some action, most probably for the first time. Decide who would end the evening as "just friends." And, most of all, appreciate the work of some true professionals who had mastered the hidden art of getting to second base with family and friends watching.

"I slow danced with the then object of my affection. It was a seminal moment for the young, undeveloped me. I still hadn't hit puberty. I was a very late bloomer."

Doug Herzog
6.3.72
Paterson, New Jersey

Lacey Schwartz
8.23.90
Seasons Restaurant
Woodstock, New York

Jill Barnett
5.2.87
Winding Hollow Country Club
Columbus, Ohio

OPEN WIDE

By SARAH SILVERMAN

I was a very late bloomer. I didn't get boobs or my period until I was seventeen. Chris Bardoff was my boyfriend most of seventh and eighth grade. The extent of our relationship was passing notes in between classes containing comments like, "Mr. Zito is giving way too much homework! Love ya, 2b 2gether 4ever, Chris." On Valentine's Day I gave him one of those giant Hershey's kisses and the Def Leppard *Pyromania* tape.

I was very queer. I had a pair of Sergio Valente jeans and a tan corduroy blazer that I would wear constantly and never wash, despite the fact that I would come back from recess soaked with sweat from playing. I also had gray corduroy knickers that I loved. I adored Paul McCartney (his solo stuff, *Pipes of Peace* and *Tug of War*). I liked Phil Collins. I'll admit it. I loved the Talking Heads. And, I was a musical theater fag.

I was madly in love with Steve Martin. I loved his comedy albums and saved all the pictures of him in magazines. I decided David Hockney was my favorite artist when I read he was Steve Martin's favorite artist.

I kissed Chris Bardoff for the first time on the dance floor in seventh grade and we pretty much only kissed while dancing, subsequently. It was open-mouthed and sloppy and sweet and totally innocent. I went home and excitedly told my dad about it, and the next morning he had my stepmother explain to me that girls who do that get reputations as sluts. This was jarring, since I was only twelve and still a professional bedwetter. I didn't do anything after that until high school, and didn't do anything more than kissing until after high school, when I officially stopped wetting the bed and became a professional slut. It's like Catholic girls. They grow up all repressed about sex, but then once the floodgates finally open, they open WIDE.

"Beth was the most crazy dangerous girl in the eighth grade because she smoked and knew stuff about philosophy. I was in lust with her from the moment she gave me a tongue kiss while playing the 'guess who's kissing you' game in a friend's backyard at a junior high party."

Jon Kesselman
1.16.88
North Hollywood, California

BURNING DOWN THE HOUSE

Hold tight. Wait till the party's over.
Hold tight. We're in for nasty weather.
—Talking Heads

The hands of the clock sweeping toward midnight signaled that the party was about to transition from a "dream come true" scenario to a scene more fitting for *Requiem for a Dream.* The wheels of the Bar Mitzvah wagon were about to fall off. Two factors were crucial in driving this. Every family has the odd uncle or two on day-release from the Betty Ford clinic who came to the day's events to witness their little angel ascend to the lofty heights of adulthood before doing their damndest to drink that bar dry. Secondly, adulthood cannot be candy coated. A crucial element of the journey toward maturity is exposure to the dark side. What better time than a Bar Mitzvah party to let the thirteen-year-old publicly try on the adult shoe of alcohol and nicotine addiction and see how well it fits?

As you peruse this gallery of derelicts and drunkards try not to judge them. It should be remembered in their defense that at this point of the evening, the die had been cast. It had already been decreed who would be getting lucky, and who would wake up in the morning asleep in the sink, a burned down cigarette in each hand, with regurgitated smatterings once on the buffet table coating the shiny pleather of their rental-tux shoes.

Jeremy Cohen
11.7.81
Montreal, Canada

THE TERRORIST

BY JIMMY JELLINEK

I grew up in the suburbs of Chicago, in a town so hebe-laden I thought that the whole world had deviated septums. As such, the Bar Mitzvah season, those heady years from seventh to eighth grade where boys become men, and if you were lucky scored a little over-the-bra tit action behind the sofas at Northmore Country Club, was a nonstop social extravaganza bar none. Yeah it was fun, if you were cool. Now granted, being cool in seventh grade is not necessarily a harbinger of things to come, but in seventh grade I was DEFINITELY UNCOOL! And not in any cool, uncool way, like being black or because I smoked or one of my parents was in jail for insider trading. I was uncool because I picked my nose and the girls called me Flinger. I was uncool because Betsy Briskman and Sussanna Burns used to sing a song that went, "Many things are ugly, but nothing's as ugly as Flinger's face." Mind you this was before Columbine and sensitivity training, so I took the abuse hard, resolving to get even by destroying each and every Bar Mitzvah I ever attended—and there were many. I started with bathroom stink bombs, the sulphuric variety that when smashed released a putrid, rotten-egg odor that overcame all comers. But this soon grew tiresome, an easy laugh that had none of the wit or flair of my later work. I naturally moved onto sight gags. There was the old "reflect the sun off the watch into the eye" trick (we didn't have laser pointers back then), which, if used to malicious effect, can cause a cantor to crumble like a *Star Trek* extra. If all else failed I just lit something on fire in the parking lot. In a few short years I managed to get myself tossed out, hollered at by hippie rabbis who played the guitar, and generally blackballed from the entire Bar Mitzvah schedule. There were mothers whose faces turned ashen at the mere sound of my voice, like Damien or Chucky, "Hi, I'm Jimmy, I'm here to destroy your son's or daughter's day." I farted during haftarahs, mooned grandparents, and smoked my first joint with the kitchen staff of Lakeshore Country Club. I became, because they made me, a one-man Bar Mitzvah Wrecking Ball. Some saw it as a cry for help. But most just thought, Ted Bundy. But I remember all their names. I know where they live. I'm watching them right know. Flinger is coming for you all.

Matt Weinberg
6.14.77
Long Island, New York

"I only know the guy—Jack was a DJ in the late seventies, a friend of my dad's. Not sure if Jack and this woman were a couple, though. I think that **Miami Vice** ***inspired the tie, it went well with an open-collared shirt, and I guess the look was Unisex."***

Matt Wood
3.15.86
The Palladium
New York, New York

"Uncle Tom is my mother's first cousin. He's a real mensch of a guy who now heads a software development company. I don't remember his speech, but I am reasonably sure it included the words 'nachas' and 'mazel.'"

Gerald Burstyn
January 1981
Holiday Inn
Evanston, Illinois

JUNGLE FEVER

Stephanie Huttner
2.28.87
The Fairmont Hotel
Denver, Colorado

When you play word association with the city of Denver, Colorado, "Bat Mitzvah" and "safari" are not the first terms that come to mind. Stephanie Huttner's safari Bat Mitzvah changed all that. Not only was this a society affair at which senators spoke, it was also a symbol of the lengths families would take to ensure party themes came to life. For "Stephanie's Safari," elephants were brought in from the Denver Zoo, snakes and tigers were airlifted from California, while animals that could not be sourced were role-played by local actors dressed up as tigers and monkeys. To ensure everyone got into the safari frame of mind, guests were asked to come dressed as if they were on an African vacation (which was easy at the time because Banana Republic was still selling clothes that looked like they'd come from an actual banana republic). And to make sure everyone kept the jungle spirit alive, each departing guest was presented with a Barbie doll dressed in Stephanie's outfit. This Bat Mitzvah is legendary in Denver, even years after the sad demise of Baby Mac the Elephant.

Adam Smith
11.5.83
Ridgeway Country Club
White Plains, New York

DANCING ON THE CEILING

People were starting to climb the walls
Ooh, it looks like everybody is having a ball
—Lionel Richie

The Village People wrote their evergreen anthem "You Can't Stop the Music" in 1982, a full four years before they played their first Bar Mitzvah gig and encountered the indomitable resistance of a Bar Mitzvah father unwilling to pay the DJ overtime. All good things come to an end, but there is little that do so with the manic quality of the Bar/Bat Mitzvah party. The dance floor smelled of sweat-soaked dress shirts, spilled drinks, and bad breath. Everyone was aware that the house lights were about to go up, the dry ice would clear, and the music was going to be pulled. The collective suspension of disbelief we had all bought into was about to come to an end and we would realize we were three hundred people covered in our own waste, standing on a flimsy wooden dance floor, in a tent, in the backyard.

Mark Melnick described this feeling most aptly as he compared the Bar Mitzvah party to a moving grill at Burger King: "Insert a well-coiffed couple, hungry and sober in one end, and voila, three hours later, emerging from the other end is a pair of exhausted drunks, hair disheveled, bloated, and minus one envelope containing thirty-six or perhaps fifty-four dollars."

Adam Smith
11.5.83
Ridgeway Country Club
White Plains, New York

Alan Bowes
2.14.87
The Pool Room, The Sheraton
Wayne, New Jersey

KISS

U got to not talk dirty, baby
If u wanna impress me
—Prince

Nothing spells sex symbol more than a thirteen-year-old at the top of his game. And so the Bar Mitzvah was the ultimate aphrodisiac. For one night only, every young man was a veritable Sean Connery around his lady classmates, and every young woman a Farrah Fawcett-Majors. Like a splash of Old Spice, the Bar Mitzvah rarely failed to do the trick, even for the most awkward of America's youth. Worn down by months of strict, almost monastic devotion to study and family, every hormone was let out for good behavior, to explode in one night of orgiastic delight. And if the youth in question was reluctant or squeamish, the Bar Mitzvah photographer was always there to dole out the assist and make sure that every album had the requisite softcore shot.

For many, the act of taking this shot was a memory they cherished for the rest of their lives, or at least until they had two girls kissing them once again. Alan Bowes (opposite) exposed some of the artifice behind the shot, which, surprisingly, was often mechanically constructed. "I remember setting up for the shot and trying to act cool. The girls seemed nonchalant about the whole thing, though. Makes me wonder whether they had done this before. Thinking back, I didn't really know them that well. In fact, I don't even think they were invited."

Andrew Goldberg
3.7.91
Mamaroneck Beach & Yacht Club
Mamaroneck, New York

Robert Cohen
6.27.82
Brooklyn, New York

Josh Weinberg
9.9.79
Woodbury Country Club
Long Island, New York

Gerald Burstyn
January 1981
Holiday Inn
Evanston, Illinios

David and Jono Kohan
4.16.77
Los Angeles, California

THE ULTIMATE APHRODISIAC

By DAVID KOHAN

In many cultures, an adolescent boy's passage from boyhood to adulthood is marked by some ritual or event. In this Jewish boy's life, that event took place at Sinai Temple during the spring of 1977, my thirteenth year. Naturally I had thought of this rite of passage many times in the months leading up to it. When the day finally arrived, I was more nervous than I ever thought I'd be, but afterwards I knew I had left my boyhood behind me. The event I'm referring to, of course, is the time my Hebrew school classmate Debbie let me put my hand down her pants in an empty classroom on the fourth floor.

Debbie was an attractive, daring girl with flashing pale eyes like a cat and a cigarette lighter bulging out the back of her Chemin de Fer jeans. She satisfied the two requirements I had for any kind of erotic association with a girl: She was willing. She was not dead.

We had started the practice of making out in empty classrooms during the ten-minute recess break sometime around the second half of Dalet. (Not coincidentally, this was about the same time that I stopped complaining to my mother that Hebrew school three times a week was excessive.) By the beginning of Hay we were ready for second base. I was picked off on my first couple of attempts, but soon I was leading my grade in stand-up doubles. (Literally. We were always standing up so we wouldn't get caught. The rationale being: It's easy to see two people groping each other while lying on the floor of an empty classroom, but two people groping each other while standing up in an empty classroom are invisible.)

One March afternoon in the year of *Saturday Night Fever*'s release, Debbie and I were fondling each other in the empty room of the very same building one goes to for moral instruction. It was there I had what alcoholics refer to as "a moment of clarity": it was time to get to third base. Why now? Perhaps it was the fact that my Bar Mitzvah was less than a month away. Or perhaps it was the words that God spoke to Moses on Mount Sinai resonating to me through the ages: "Go Down!" But most likely it was the fact that Debbie herself had undone the top button of her jeans. Naturally, a gentleman has to omit the details about what happened next. Anyway, so she's got her pants unbuttoned, and I'm thinking, "This is it!" At which point I suavely banged my head against the pointy part of the metal eraser shelf very, very hard. The pain was so intense that I started to sweat profusely from the effort to suppress it. I smiled wanly at Debbie. Not because I had the inclination to smile, but rather because the skin around the corners of my mouth was being pulled upwards by the lump that was forming on the back of my head. She said, "Ooh, are you okay?" "Yurp," I replied. It was magic.

Eric Rubenstein
2.5.84
Tamarac, Florida

The feeling I had afterward was everything I imagined my post–Bar Mitzvah feeling would be. The sense that a Rubicon had been crossed. That I had been afforded the opportunity to have an adult experience, and everything was now a little bit different. I felt more mature, a little superior to my classmates who had yet to experience it, and a little bit woozy. The parallels between my experience with Debbie and my Bar Mitzvah are striking to me now. Both events took place in the spring of 1977 at Sinai Temple. Both felt like a line of demarcation between childhood and not-childhood. One was a religious coming-of-age. The other was a sexual coming-of-age. One was the greatest thing that can happen to a Jewish boy and the crowning achievement of the first thirteen years of my life. The other was my Bar Mitzvah.

Ari Osur
6.13.87
Fairfield Sheraton
Fairfield, New Jersey

Josh Kun
8.18.84
Los Angeles, California

"The Corvette was the photographer's car. It was his idea to take this shot. My dad was livid about the photograph. He said, 'No wonder the guy charges so much — look at his car.' The only thing on my mind was getting back inside for another round of Huggie Bear."

Michelle Shapiro
11.2.86
Battleground Country Club
Freehold, New Jersey

NEVER CAN SAY GOODBYE

Every time I think I've had enough
And start heading for the door
—Jackson Five

Saying goodbye is never easy, especially when you are forced to do so on the hoarsely barked command of an impatient photographer desperate to blow the show and get home by one A.M. The delicate goodbye wave is the final classic in every Bar/Bat Mitzvah album. The boy or girl has come to the end of the road. The speeches have been made, the candles have burned down, the guests have danced themselves out, and the confetti cannons have blown their load. The guest of honor bids us a gentle adieu. The door is half open. The question is, are they waving goodbye to childhood or hello to adulthood? Either way, they still have a ten o'clock weekend curfew and no pubic hair.

A little-known fact about this particular shot is that it was normally taken hours before the party ever began. Look again and you will see, in most cases, the evening's star is still squeaky clean, a little itchy for the night to begin, and forced to feign exhaustion as if the whole shebang was already over. The one true candid of the lot is the shot of poor Dad, looking directly into the camera even as he desperately rushes through the arithmetic of how he will reshuffle his pension plan to finance this one night of majesty and magic.

Jeffrey Bartha
4.27.85
Mamaroneck Beach & Yacht Club
Mamaroneck, New York

Sarra Cooper
5.18.91
Middle Bay Country Club
Oceanside, New York

Lisa Rosenblum
4.29.89
Radisson Suites
Palm Beach Gardens, Florida

Andrew Goldberg
3.7.91
Mamaroneck Beach & Yacht Club
Mamaroneck, New York

Anonymous
circa 1968
Queens, New York

WHERE ARE THEY NOW?

MIKE EPSTEIN is the vice president of Epstein Funeral Directors.

SCOTT JACOBY is a singer/songwriter and music producer living in New York. One of his songs is presently at the top of the charts in Japan.

JAMIE GLASSMAN has recovered from his bullied youth to become a writer/producer for the *Ali G* show in England.

KATE LEE is a literary agent in New York.

JILL BARNETT is an elementary school teacher in the town she is pointing to on the map—Columbus, Ohio.

DARA OSUR (back, far left) used to work in the entertainment industry and currently lives in Los Angeles, California.

ABBEY ORLOFSKY is an investment banker in the Boston area.

EILEEN QUAST is stuck in her adolescent years working as a communications manager at MTV. She lives with her husband Dave in TriBeCa.

REBECCA RUBENSTEIN is a CPA and is shown here in her wedding dress, which fortunately was not inspired by a music video.

MATT WEINBERG lives on the Lower East Side of Manhattan. He makes people smile by selling wonderful chocolates, coffees, salad dressings, and other gifty gourmets.

JOSHUA WEINBERG is living in San Francisco, where he works as a high-tech PR consultant.

ANDREW GOLDBERG lives in Los Angeles and works on the critically acclaimed TV show *The Family Guy.*

SAMANTHA AND JEN CORWIN are as close as ever living together in Manhattan. Samantha is a special education teacher, and Jennifer is a vice president in derivatives at an investment bank.

DOUG HERZOG is president of Comedy Central and Spike TV.

ELISSA STEIN is a New York writer, illustrator, and graphic designer.

JASON SILVERMAN now lives in Israel with his wife and child.

JON KESSELMAN is a Los Angeles–based writer/director whose credits include the first Jewxploitation film, *The Hebrew Hammer.*

JOSH KUN is a professor and journalist whose writings have appeared in *The New York Times, Los Angeles Times,* and a number of other publications.

JORDANA WINTON CASCIANO is a public official in the village in which she resides.

JORDAN CARLOS is a New York City comedian who is too scared to leave the security of his full-time job as a copywriter.

MARK RONSON is DJ/music producer living in New York City.

STEPHANIE HUTTNER lives with her husband, Ira Kleinman, in Little Rock.

MICHELLE SHAPIRO is a marketing and communications consultant.

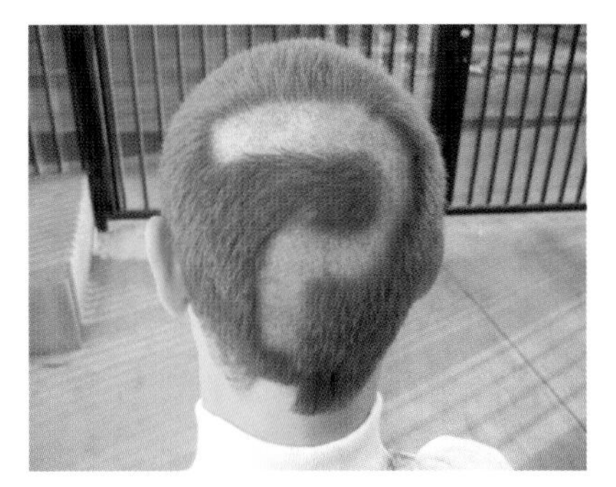

SAM SPIEGEL, a.k.a. DJ Squeak E. Clean, spends most of his time helping the needy children of Bel Aire.

ADAM, ZACHARY, AND JONATHAN (JJ) SMITH live in New York and are in real estate, public policy and finance respectively.

WENDY McSWAIN in her signature Bar/Bat Mitzvah dress, which she returned to Macy's years later without the receipt.

Cultural critics have long debated the exact impact MTV has had on our generation. Less known is the impact Bat and Bar Mitzvahs have had on MTV during its fledgling years. We want to both tell the story and in doing so, thank **Wendy McSwain,** for her support over the lifetime of the project. Wendy worked on Club MTV, which launched the glittering careers of star dancers such as Camille Donatacci and Jennifer Esposito. But when corporate America doesn't pay the bills, where do you turn? The Bat Mitzvah circuit of Long Island of course. The job of chaperoning the moonlighting dancers to two or three gigs a night befell her, and what an eye-opener it was. The first party she arrived at, a forty-foot neon-encrusted MTV logo descended from the rafters to announce their dance troupe's arrival. "My gut reaction was one of indignation. Who authorized the use of the logo? Then I calmed down and was in awe of everything I saw. The brilliance, the exuberance, the gaudiness of it all." The mixture was intoxicating and impossible to resist. Within weeks, Wendy was donning a specially procured outfit, topping it all off with a pair of false "Liza Lashes," and joining in the act with a storming set of show ballads ending in a brutal but crowd-pleasing rendition of "Through the Eyes of Love" the famed theme from the movie *Ice Castles.*

Contributors

One of the pleasures of creating this book has been working with the slew of writers, journalists, and comedians who were up for the challenge of taking a wander down Bar Mitzvah memory lane with us. We are grateful to each and every one of the following who chose to save the money they would have spent in therapy by sharing their stories with the great American public:

Amber Bonadio lives in Monterey, California, and was born in Scranton, Pennsylvania. She is a graduate of the U.S. Naval Academy.

Jordan Carlos is the preppiest black guy in the free world. He was born and raised in Dallas, Texas, and lives in New York City, where he is a writer and comedian.

Eric Drysdale is a New York–based comedian and writer. He's been on TV a couple of times, which is very exciting to his mother.

Jonathan Safran Foer is the author of *Everything Is Illuminated* and *Extremely Loud and Incredibly Close: A Novel.*

Brett Gelman is an actor/comedian in New York City. He is one half of the hip-hop juggernaut Cracked Out.

Scott M. Gimple lives in Southern California and is best known for creating a cartoon called *Fillmore!,* writing the comic *Heroes Anonymous,* and his amazing soups.

Matt Goldich is a writer and stand-up comedian who performs regularly all over New York City.

Peter Hyman is the author of *The Reluctant Metrosexual: Dispatches from an Almost Hip Life* as well as numerous journalistic articles on culture you've likely never seen.

AJ Jacobs is a senior editor at *Esquire* magazine. He is the author of *The Know It All: One Man's Humble Quest to Become the Smartest Guy in the World.* He lives in New York City.

Jimmy Jellinek is the editor-in-chief of *Complex* magazine.

Jessi Klein is a New York City–bred comedian and writer who has appeared on Comedy Central, MTV, VH1, CNN and CNBC. She is the director of development for Comedy Central, and is an executive on *Chappelle's Show* and *Insomniac with David Attell.*

David Kohan is the creator and executive producer of *Will & Grace.* He lives and works in Los Angeles and has a twin who made exactly the same mistakes in exactly the same places as he did during his Bar Mitzvah recitation.

Josh Kun is a Los Angeles writer and critic who teaches in the English Department at University California Riverside. He is the author of *Audiotopia: Music, Race, and America* and co-editor of forthcoming collections about David Mamet's interior decorating skills and the Jewish mambo craze of the 1950s. He is also a founding member of Reboot Stereophonic, a specialty label dedicated to excavating Jewish musical alternatives.

David Measer grew up in West Los Angeles, where he played on Little League baseball teams with the children of some of the most powerful people in Hollywood. He spent his twenties working for opera companies in Europe, and has since returned to L.A., where he works in advertising.

Mark Ronson is a DJ and producer in New York City. He has produced or remixed Nikka Cost, Air, Jay Z, Sean Paul, and Jimmy Fallon. He released his own debut album, *Here Comes the Fuzz,* last year on Elektra and has just started a label, Allido Records.

Sarah Silverman is a comic/writer/actress. She's pretty and has black hair.

Sam Spiegel is a superstar DJ and producer. After a failed career in competitive swimming, he eradicated the leprosy epidemic in Bombay, and then moved to LA, where he now resides.

Shaun Sperling lives and works in Chicago and is still as nice a Jewish boy as he was at his Bar Mitzvah.

Wendy Spero is a comedian/actress who has appeared on Comedy Central, VH1, Oxygen, and NBC. She was named "Best Female Stand-up of 2003" by *Time Out New York.*

Joel Stein was Bar Mitzvahed at Temple Emanuel in New Jersey, where the keyboardist for Bon Jovi was also Bar Mitzvahed. He went to Stanford, was a staff writer for *Time* magazine, and is now an op-ed columnist for the *LA Times.*

Noah Tepperberg is the co-owner of a marketing/special events firm called Strategic Marketing Group and a nightclub/event space called Marquee, both located in New York.

Jon Wagner is a New York City–based writer who was born in Washington, DC.

David Wain is a New York comedian and filmmaker. His work includes the MTV series *The State,* the feature film *Wet Hot American Summer,* and the comedy trio STELLA.

Ali Waller is a writer and comedian living in New York and working on staff at *Saturday Night Live.*

Gideon Yago is a nice Jewish boy from Queens who works for basic cable. He didn't get any at his own Bar Mitzvah, or for that matter, until he was about sixteen.

Photographers

This book would not have been possible if not for the amazing men and women who've dedicated their professional lives to the art of Bar and Bat Mitzvah photography. Just like many of the checks and presents received at Bar Mitzvahs, not every photographer could be accounted for. Please contact us to be included in any future printings of this book.

Steven Kormes Inc., Pinto Studios, Lorn Spolter, Bass Photo, Fred Marcus Photography, Harold Hechler Photography, Peter Chernin, Lawrence Lesser, Jerry Lord, Sherry Bakhtiar, Conrad Mulcahy, Knight and Deutsch Photography, Alan and Alan Photography, Steve Merzer, Florida Portriats, Shayn Studios, Allan Reider Studio, Barry Brown Studios, Orly Halevy, Curtis Dahl Photography, Conrad Mulcahy

Acknowledgments

We are deeply indebted to the hundreds of thousands of people who have vibed with us through our website over the past eighteen months. Your photos, stories, table centerpieces, encouragement, and criticism have been unbelievable.

Thanks to all those who have helped us pull this book off technically. Sam Ottenhoff at Longsight and Erica Cordier for their web assistance. Michael Cohen at Death, Dumb, and Blind Communications, and Josh Kun, whose knowledge of eighties song lyrics are as deep as the ocean. Jan Frank, Yitka Wayne, and Zsolt Sarvary-Bene for their photographic work. Conrad Mulcahy for his photographic genius everywhere else. Michael Sukin and Roberta Korus for their legal guidance. Mireille Silcoff, Daniel Bronstein, *Spin* magazine and Gawker.com for spreading the word so quickly. The following should be singled out for their strategic and creative advice at different junctures: Josh Neuman at Crush, Seth Rodsky at CAA and Strategic Group, David Katznelson at Birdman, Daniel Seliger, Lyle Owerko, Ron at Smartbomb, Scott Belsky, Michael Ian Kaye MIA, and James Spindler.

We are immensely indebted to all of the characters who rose to the challenge and took us on a trip back in time through their essays. Especially Jonathan Safran Foer, AJ Jacobs, David Kohan, Noah Tepperberg, Jessi Klein, Mark Ronson, and Joel Stein, who seemingly turned theirs around overnight.

We would love to single out the following for their photographic endeavors extraordinaire: Jon Kesselman, Stacy Marcus, Catie Lazarus, Stephanie Huttner (you amaze), Ben Lee, Julie Weitz, the Orlofskys, Marla Garfield (who took several trips back to Michigan to dig out her stuff), Julie Hermelin (ditto), Doug Herzog, and all at Comedy Central, Stephen Freidman at MtvU, and El Saeso for his unceasing support and introducing us to Russ at SSUR and A-ron at aNYthing.

Finally, we would like to thank our agents Kate Lee and Richard Abate at ICM, who are both passionate and strategic. All the staff at Crown kick ass. Doug Pepper connected with us at the outset, and our editor, Carrie Thornton, with the assistance of Orly Trieber, led the project in ways we would never have dreamt about. Lauren Dong is an icon. Thanks also to Kay Schuckhart, Mark McCauslin, and Felix Gregorio.

Roger Bennett would like to thank: Samuel Polak, who dug books, chess, history, and America; Valerie and Ivor Bennett; Nigel, Rebecca, Amy, and Holly (1991–2004); all of the Dvorsky family; Vanessa and Samson Hy, who were so supportive, patient, insightful, loving, patient, and forgiving; late greats: Mrs. Barton, Mrs. Lindsay, and Mrs. Simpson; Lew Kreinberg, Norman Rosenberg, and Robyn Kramer, for their mentorship; AYEMBEE and SEEAREBEE and all the staff at ACBP who have supported us in every possible way from the outset. Jeffrey Solomon is the coolest gent above the age of fifty in America today. No contest; Rachel Levin, total genius; Daniel Harverd and the gents who run the Talisker Distillery on the Isle of Skye; Karen Ush, who rocks so hard; the Kroll

Family and Celia Dollar; and Jamie Glassman from the sandbox to the grave. Finally, Prentice Minner and the staff at the Kutshers Hotel, who have inspired and encouraged us without ever knowing it, the waiters at Gino's, Marvin, Freddie Roman, Steve-O, Joey Cora, Everton Football Club, Badly Drawn Boy, and Shellby Lynn.

Jules Shell would like to thank: Nanny for the precious contents in her cabinets and the foresight to save everything. Mom and Dad for going over and beyond and learning how to use the scanner. Deb, Leen, Dave, Gram and Gramps. ZSB for more than you will ever know. Mr. Ralston, Kathy Moskal and Bob McCord, the Solfanellis, Uncle Ira, Murray Katcher, Ira Kane, Betty Bartha, Sally Brown, the amazing Wendy McSwain, Margaux Baran, and Nina, Danny, Walter, and Naomi for sharing their love of documentary photography. Seth Singerman for not holding a grudge over the Vuarnets in the lake incident. The Sassers, DDursch, Rita Kusuma for her early conversations. Buzz Alexander, Susan Winer, Louise Freyman, Dennis Watlington, and Bruce Gilbert, for being out of the box early on. Gerasimos and the waitstaff at the Chelsea Gallery Restaurant. Loren Spalter, Mike, Brett, Shari, Jill, Lindsay, Elissa, Alan, Sam, Jen, and the Shell, Cohen and Adler cousins—and all those who willingly entrusted us with their albums. And to those who are larger than life and have colored my world with the most fantastical stories: Rosalie Gwathmey, Mr. Wickham, Freddie Roman, Alan and Joyce, Ernie the handyman, Mrs. Moore, Annie Hampton, Auntie Moo, Uncle Sam, Super Nana, and my grandfather Max.

Nick Kroll would like to thank: My mother, Lynn Kroll, for paving the way for Jewish mothers everywhere to take their sacred Bar Mitzvah albums out of the safe confines of their bookshelves; the whole of the Kroll Family: Dad, Jeremy, Dana, Vanessa, Nicky, and the li'l ones for their undying support, and Nana for being the only grandma with whom you can talk about sex. The NYC comedy community—specifically Owen Burke and the Upright Citizens Brigade, Chelsea Peretti, Roger Hailes, Jordan Carlos, Brett Gelman, Mike Birbiglia, Ed Herro, John Mulaney, Jake Fleischer, Brian Donovan, Todd Womack, Jessi Klein, Dan Powell, and the entire Comedy Central Development Office. Eric Drysdale for not only contributing to the book but for helping us early on with a link from his fantastic website. There were a number of families who trusted us with their memories before anyone knew they could trust us: the Jacoby family, the Chadakoff family, the Goldbergs, the Benerofe crew, and the Seigels. A couple of characters who found us who we have come to love: Mark Melnick and Elliott Goldkind. Matt Issembert, Sarra Cooper, Matt Wood for providing us with a plethora of beautiful pictures. Howard Bragman for showing us how one quote can make a book come alive. Thanks to my agents at Atlas Talent for making my schedule so flexible. Alan Kanoff and Pam Friedman for their advice and assistance, Adina Erem of *Lifestyles* magazine for her help in connecting us to amazing Bar Mitzvah photographers. And most important, to the '86 Mets, who showed us all that you can drink martinis in the clubhouse and still win championships.

THE ENCHANTED EVENT
100
ISES
(516) 467-6628
INTERNATIONAL SPECIAL EVENTS SOCIETY
ENCHANTED PARTIES OF AMERICA
ONE HUNDRED MEMORIES
President
STEVE FORTGANG ENTERTAINING ORCHESTRA
King of The Court
Jeff
I JUST DID IT at KENNY'S BAR MITZVAH!
DECEMBER 7,1991
MEMORIES OF MY BAR MITZVAH
STEPPIN' OUT WITH
AMI
JUNE 2, 1990
SCOTT
BENJAMIN
Miriam
Brace Yourself!
for Daniella's Bat Mitzvah
I Got to 2nd Base
at Jonah's Bar Mitzvah!
A WALLET FOR YOUR
Bar Mitzvah
STEVE FORTGANG . . . THE No. 1 BAR MITZVAH BAND